Copyright © 2025 by Holly Symons
All rights reserved.

No part of this book may be reproduced, scanned, or distributed in any printed or electronic form without permission.
This book is a work of fiction. Names, characters, places, and incidents are either the product of the author's imagination or used fictitiously.
Hardback - ISBN: 978-1-923567-45-0
Paperback - ISBN: 978-1-923567-46-7
eBook - ISBN: 978-1-923567-47-4

Cover design by **Holly Symons**
First Edition

For More, Please Visit
HollySymons.com.au

"Warning: Contains 0% tolerance for breadcrumbers and 100% permission to ghost the Gingerbread Man."

Gingerbread Man

Is the kind of book women can laugh at while crying into their wine glass, thinking,

"Yup, I dated or married that cookie, too."

~

Run, run as fast as you can, you don't want him if he's a Gingerbread Man.

Gingerbread Man

A Girlfriend's Guide to Avoiding Men Who Breadcrumb

First Addition

HOLLY SYMONS

This book is intended for educational and self-help purposes only. It is not a substitute for professional therapy, counselling, or medical advice. If you are struggling with your mental health, please seek support from a qualified professional.

Author's Note (Trigger Warning + Support)

This book talks honestly about toxic relationships, family dynamics, and emotional struggles. Some chapters may bring up strong or unexpected feelings. If at any point you feel overwhelmed, please pause, take a breath, and reach out for support - you do not have to go through it alone.

Free, confidential help is available:

- **AUSTRALIA: Lifeline** – Call 13 11 14 or text 0477 13 11 14
- **UK & IRELAND:** Samaritans – Call 116 123 (freephone)
- **USA & CANADA:** 988 Suicide & Crisis Lifeline – Call or text 988

Gingerbread Men, Crumbs & How to Stop Eating Them

PART ONE: CRUMBS, CHAOS & CONFUSION 1
1. WHAT IS BREADCRUMBING (AND WHY IT'S NOT FLIRTING) 2
2. THE GINGERBREAD MEN YOU'LL MEET – A FIELD GUIDE 4
3. CRUMBS IN THE DMS: HOW MODERN DATING GOT SO LAZY 7
4. LOVE BOMBING VS. ACTUAL INTEREST: WHY YOU'RE CONFUSED 10
5. EMOTIONAL INFLATION: WHY "I MISS YOU" IS WORTH 5 CENTS NOW 13
6. TEXTING GYMNASTICS – THE DOUBLE BACKFLIP OF "SORRY I'VE BEEN BUSY" 16
7. WHEN A MEME IS NOT A LOVE LANGUAGE 19
8. "WE'RE JUST VIBING" AND OTHER RED FLAGS DRESSED AS CHILL 22
9. HE SAYS HE'S "NOT READY" BUT WANTS TO CUDDLE? SIR. 25
10. IS HE HEALING OR HIDING? A GUIDE TO THE EMOTIONALLY UNAVAILABLE 28
11. THE "I'M NOT LIKE OTHER GUYS" STARTER PACK 31
12. SWEET TALK & VANISHING ACTS – WELCOME TO THE CRUMB PARADE 34

13. How to Spot Breadcrumbs Before the First Date   37
14. Red Flags Disguised as Spontaneous Road Trips   40
15. The Chase Game (And Why It's Designed to Drain You)   43
16. I Don't Think He's Busy, Babe - I Think He's Boring   45

PART TWO: Crumb Connoisseurs Anonymous   48

16. How to Rewire Your Heart So You Stop Craving Crumbs   49
17. What Your Brain Thinks Breadcrumbs Mean (It's Wrong)   51
18. But We Had a Vibe – Trauma, Fantasy, and Misread Energy   54
19. Did I Fall or Was I Pushed? The Illusion of Connection   57
20. Girl Math – If He Texted You After 3 Days, Is That Love?   60
21. The Almost Relationship and Its Emotional Hangover   63
22. How to Know You're Trauma-Bonded to a Ghost   65
22. How to Know You're Trauma-Bonded to a Ghost   68
23. If You're in His Phone, As Maybe You're Not   71
24. Did He Actually Do Anything Wrong, or Am I Just Starving?   73
25. You're Not Crazy, He's Just Inconsistent   76
26. The Power of Blocking – Digitally and Emotionally   79
27. Inner Child Needs a Snack, Not a Crumb Man   82

28. You Don't Want Him, You Want Closure 85
29. When You Romanticise Red Flags and Call It Chemistry 88
30. He's Not Deep, He's Just Avoidant with a Spotify Playlist 91

PART THREE: Red Flags, Replays & Reckonings **93**

31. Red Flags Disguised as Spontaneous Road Trips 94
32. He's Just Bad at Texting and Other Lies I Told Myself 96
33. Do You Like Him or Just the Way He Held That Coffee? 99
34. He Calls You Babe but Forgets Your Birthday 101
35. The Guy Who Cries During Sex and Disappears by Morning 103
36. Men Who Do Yoga and Still Ghost You 106
37. The Guy with an Audi and No Emotional Depth 109
38. He Had Crystals and a Co-Star App, But Still Breadcrumbed Me 111
39. I'm Just Focusing on Me (While Actively Leading You On) 114
40. The Man Who Asked for My Netflix Password Mid-Breakup 116
41. Why He's Obsessed with You but Still Not Dating You 118
42. The Spiritual One Who Said He Was Processing for 7 Months 121
43. The Guy Who Gave You a Nickname but Not a Label 123
44. He Said He Missed Me… Then Replied 8 Days Later 125

45. IF YOU THINK HE MIGHT BE IN A SITUATIONSHIP, YOU ARE 127
PART FOUR: ESCAPE PLANS & GLOW-UPS 129
46. GETTING THE HELL OUT WITHOUT TEXTING "U UP?" FIRST 130
47. DON'T BLOCK TO GET A REACTION, BLOCK TO GET PEACE 132
48. THE BREAKUP IS THE CLOSURE 134
49. A GLOW-UP ISN'T JUST LIP GLOSS, IT'S SELF-RESPECT 136
50. DELETE THE CHAT, NOT JUST THE CONTACT 138
51. YOU'RE NOT TOO SENSITIVE, YOU'RE JUST FINALLY LISTENING TO YOURSELF 140
52. STOP TEXTING HIM. HE'S A CRUMB 142
53. YOU CAN'T HEAL WHERE YOU'RE BEING HURT 144
54. IF HE WANTED TO, HE WOULD (AND HE HASN'T BABE) 146
55. DON'T LET THE MEMES FOOL YOU. THAT'S NOT COMMUNICATION 148
56. LET THEM MISS YOU FROM THE BLOCK LIST 150
57. YOU CAN BE HORNY AND HAVE BOUNDARIES 152
58. HEAL SO YOU DON'T WRITE HIM INTO YOUR NEXT STORY 154
59. YOU'RE NOT A MYSTERY TO BE SOLVED, YOU'RE A STANDARD TO BE MET 156
60. FROM FERAL TO FABULOUS – A POST-CRUMB COMEBACK PLAN 158
PART FIVE: THE GINGERBREAD MEN ARCHIVES 161
61. THE TIME HE SENT ME A PLAYLIST INSTEAD OF APOLOGISING 162
62. A MAN GAVE ME A ROCK. NOT A RING. JUST… A ROCK 164

63. I Asked What We Were, and He Said I Thought We Were Vibes	166
64. I'm Not Emotionally Ready While Planning Our Future Vacay	168
65. He Asked Me to Babysit His Dog, Then Dated Someone Else	170
66. My Crumb Man Said I Was Too Empowered	172
67. I Found Out I Was the Side Quest	174
68. We Matched Dated Ghosted Matched Again	176
69. He Took Me to IKEA and Never Spoke Again	178
70. The One Who Said You're Like a Sister to Me After Sex	180
71. I Met His Family Before I Met His Commitment	182
72. He Complimented My Boundaries Then Crossed Every One	184
73. The Date Who Cried About His Ex Then Asked for Nudes	186
74. I Thought It Was a Relationship. He Thought It Was Thursday	188
75. We Should See Other People, Bro, I Haven't Seen You	191
PART SIX: LOVE WITHOUT CRUMBS	**193**
76. What Real Commitment Actually Feels Like	194
77. How to Spot the Green Flags Before You Miss Them	196
78. Trust Isn't Earned Through Vibes, It's Built Through Action	199
78. Trust Isn't Earned Through Vibes, It's Built Through Action	201

79. HE TEXTS BACK, HE SHOWS UP, THAT'S IT. THAT'S THE STANDARD　203
80. NO MIXED SIGNALS, NO CRUMBS, JUST CONSISTENCY　205
81. LOVE SHOULDN'T FEEL LIKE A MYSTERY NOVEL　207
82. DON'T ROMANTICISE CONFUSION, THAT'S NOT LOVE　209
83. HEALTHY LOVE IS BORING AT FIRST, AND THAT'S HOT　211
84. YOU DON'T HAVE TO HEAL TO BE LOVED, YOU JUST HAVE TO BE SAFE　213
85. REWRITE YOUR FANTASY TO MATCH YOUR FUTURE　215
86. LET THEM GO SO THE RIGHT ONE CAN KNOCK　218
87. YOU ARE NOT TOO MUCH, YOU'VE JUST OUTGROWN CRUMBS　220
88. LOVE WILL FEEL LIKE COMING HOME, NOT LIKE BEING TESTED　222
89. YOU DON'T NEED CLOSURE, YOU NEED DISTANCE　224
90. THE HAPPILY EVER AFTER YOU WROTE FOR THEM? WRITE IT FOR YOU　226
91. HOW TO SET BOUNDARIES WITHOUT SOUNDING LIKE A TED TALK　229
92. LOVING SOMEONE DOESN'T MEAN YOU OWE THEM ACCESS　229
93. YOU'RE NOT CRAZY, YOU'RE BEING MANIPULATED　230
94. HOW TO SAY THIS ISN'T ENOUGH AND MEAN IT　230
95. IF YOU HAVE TO BEG FOR THE BARE MINIMUM, IT'S NOT LOVE　231

96. WHY YOU KEEP MAKING EXCUSES FOR HIM
(AND HOW TO STOP) 231
97. YOU CAN'T CHANGE HIM WITH LOVE. HE'S NOT
A FIXER UPPER 232
98. WHEN YOU WANT TO LEAVE BUT STILL HOPE
HE'LL GET IT 232
99. YOU'RE NOT MEAN FOR HAVING NEEDS 233
100. HOW TO LOVE HIM WITHOUT LOSING
YOURSELF 233
101. YOU DON'T NEED TO BE PERFECT TO DESERVE
RESPECT 234
102. HE DOESN'T HAVE TO HIT YOU TO HURT YOU
234
103. WHEN APOLOGIES TURN INTO MANIPULATION
235
104. HE'S NOT THAT BAD IS NOT A JUSTIFICATION
235
105. YOU CAN'T HEAL IN THE SAME PLACE THAT
HURT YOU 236
106. IF YOU HAVE TO CONVINCE HIM TO STAY,
HE'S ALREADY GONE 236
107. STOP EDITING YOURSELF TO BE EASIER TO
LOVE 237
108. YOU'RE NOT DRAMATIC, YOU'RE JUST DONE
BEING IGNORED 237
109. HOW TO SET A BOUNDARY WITHOUT
APOLOGISING AFTER 238
110. SAVE THE SCREENSHOT, NOT THE
RELATIONSHIP 238
ABOUT THE AUTHOR **333**
GINGERBREAD MAN: A GIRLFRIEND'S GUIDE
PLAYLIST **334**

PART ONE:
Crumbs, Chaos & Confusion

1. What Is Breadcrumbing (and Why It's Not Flirting)

Breadcrumbing is when someone gives you *just enough* attention to keep you hooked, but never enough to actually feed the relationship. Think of it like a bakery that lures you in with the smell of fresh bread, hands you one stale crumb, then closes the door and tells you to "be patient, babe."

It's not flirting, it's emotional stringing. Flirting has intent, momentum, and the possibility of something real. Breadcrumbing has a broken compass, a half-charged phone, and no plans to meet you anywhere other than the land of confusion.

The danger? Your brain starts mistaking crumbs for cake. You find yourself analysing emojis like it's the Da Vinci Code, holding onto "Hey stranger" texts like they're handwritten love letters, and waiting for the next crumb drop like a famished pigeon in a city park.

Here's the thing: if he wanted to be with you, you wouldn't be wondering. If you're *always* wondering, that's the answer.

2. The Gingerbread Men You'll Meet – A Field Guide

Not all crumb-sprinklers are created equal. Some are flaky from the start, others start out as a full loaf before slowly turning into dust. Knowing which type you've met isn't about *excusing* them, it's about recognising the pattern before you're three months deep in voice notes and confusion.

Here's your **Crumb Criminal Line-Up**:

1. **The Weekend Baker**
    - Only appears Friday night through Sunday morning. Vanishes the rest of the week like carbs during a fad diet.
2. **The "Just Checking In" Crumbler**

- His texts have the nutritional value of a Tic Tac. "Hey" … "U up?" … "Thinking of you" (at 1:12 a.m.).

3. **The Long-Distance Loafer**
    - Lives close enough to see you, but insists *life is just so busy right now*. Loves to FaceTime from bed but never leaves his postcode for you.

4. **The Social Media Chef**
    - Double-taps every photo, comments with the occasional flame emoji, but hasn't asked you out since the Jurassic era.

5. **The Future Faker Baker**

- Talks about your wedding playlist before you've even had coffee together. Never actually plans a date.

6. **The "Work's Been Crazy" Bun**
    - Always too busy to hang out… but somehow has time for golf, beers with the boys, and his mum's roast lamb every Sunday.

7. **The Seasonal Scone**
    - Disappears when it's cold, comes back when it's beach weather, ready to "reconnect" just in time for summer selfies.

Bottom line: These guys don't offer a meal, just enough to keep you nibbling. And you, my love, deserve the five-course tasting menu.

3. Crumbs in the DMs: How Modern Dating Got So Lazy

Once upon a time, courtship meant candlelit dinners, hand-written letters, and awkwardly meeting someone's parents' way too soon. Now? It's "wyd?" in your DMs at 11:47 p.m. and an occasional fire emoji on your Instagram Story.

Breadcrumbing has gone digital, and honestly, it's never been easier for a man to do the absolute bare minimum while still convincing you he's "putting in effort."

The Lazy Love Language of DMs:

- **The Emoji Drive-By** – No words, just emojis like he's playing charades instead of starting a conversation.

- **The Reply Guy** – Pops up only when you post something thirst-trap adjacent. Disappears when you actually reply.
- **The Meme Dealer** – Sends you memes without context, so it *feels* like bonding, but you realise you know more about his sense of humour than his actual personality.
- **The Double Tap Phantom** – Likes every post, never sends a message. Like a polite ghost who haunts your feed.

The problem? The dopamine hit from those tiny interactions tricks your brain into thinking there's a real connection forming. But there's a big difference between *attention* and *intention*. One lasts a second, the other builds a relationship.

If his energy is "quick reaction emoji" instead of "actual conversation," babe, you're not dating you're just a pit stop on his scroll.

4. Love Bombing vs. Actual Interest: Why You're Confused

At first, love bombing feels like you've finally won the dating lottery.

He's texting "Good morning, beautiful" before you've even opened your eyes, sending flowers "just because," and talking about your future together like he's got a Pinterest board titled *Our Wedding*.

But here's the plot twist: love bombing isn't about *you*. It's about control. It's an emotional sugar rush that gets you hooked fast only for the crash to hit when his attention suddenly evaporates.

The Love Bombing Cycle:

1. **Intense Pursuit** – He's everywhere. Calls, texts, gifts, affection. You feel seen, adored, and chosen.
2. **Emotional Overwhelm** – It's so much, so fast, that your brain skips over healthy caution and straight into *maybe this is The One.*
3. **The Shift** – Once you're invested, the energy drops. Messages slow down. Plans get vague. You're left chasing the high you felt in week one.

How to Tell Its Genuine Interest Instead:

- Effort is steady, not spiky.
- They respect your boundaries instead of steamrolling them "because we're so close already."

- Future talk comes with *actions*, not just poetic text messages at midnight.

Bottom line: Love should feel warm and consistent, not like an emotional rollercoaster with a gift shop exit. If the grand gestures vanish the moment you feel safe, babe, it wasn't love, it was bait.

5. Emotional Inflation: Why "I Miss You" Is Worth 5 Cents Now

There was a time when "I miss you" meant something. It meant someone had actually noticed your absence, thought about you, and wanted you near. Now? It's become the clearance-bin Hallmark card of dating — overused, under-delivered, and worth about five cents in emotional currency.

Why it's lost its value:

- It's often sent as a placeholder instead of making real plans.
- It's become the go-to line when they feel you pulling away, just enough to keep you hooked.

- In the age of instant communication, "missing" someone lasts about as long as a TikTok trend.

Translation Guide:

- "I miss you" after days of silence = *I noticed you stopped chasing me and I'd like my ego boost back.*
- "I miss you" at 2 a.m. = *I'm lonely and scrolling my options.*
- "I miss you" without a follow-up invite = *I miss the idea of you, not the effort it takes to see you.*

The Fix:

Don't get starry-eyed over words that aren't backed by consistent action. If he really misses you, you won't just hear it, you'll see it in the plans he makes, the effort he gives, and the way he shows up.

Remember: In a world full of inflated words, actions are the only currency that hold value.

6. Texting Gymnastics – The Double Backflip of "Sorry I've Been Busy"

Ah, the classic "Sorry I've been busy" text, the Olympic sport of dodging accountability while still pretending to care.

How it works:

He disappears for days, sometimes weeks, then swings back in with an apologetic flourish like he's been climbing Everest without Wi-Fi. The goal? To make you feel *understanding* instead of noticing the gaping hole where consistent effort should be.

The Common Routines:

- **The Triple Twist Excuse:** "Sorry, I've been busy with work/family/my dog's anxiety."
- **The Phantom Flirt:** Drops back in with a compliment so you forget you were mad.
- **The Emotional Somersault:** Shares a personal struggle to reset the emotional playing field and earn your sympathy.
- **The Busy-Busy Double:** Disappears *again* right after "making it up to you."

Why it works (on them, not on us):

Humans are wired to be polite and forgiving especially if we're already emotionally invested. They're betting you'll accept the excuse, reset the clock, and keep them in rotation.

Your Power Move:

The next time someone tries a "Sorry I've been busy" double backflip, remember you're not the judge holding up a scorecard. You're the prize they should be showing up for without acrobatics.

If their "busy" always leaves you waiting, it's not a scheduling conflict; it's a priority conflict.

7. When a Meme Is Not a Love Language

Don't get me wrong, a well-timed meme can be cute. It can say, *I saw this and thought of you.* But when memes are the **only** thing holding your conversations together? Babe, you're in a situationship powered by recycled internet content.

Why it feels like connection:

- Memes are funny, relatable, and make you feel seen in the moment.
- They create micro-bursts of interaction without the effort of actual conversation.

- They trick your brain into thinking he's engaging when really, he's outsourcing his personality to Instagram.

The Meme Relationship Types:

1. **The Serial Forwarder** – Sends you 15 TikToks in a row, doesn't respond when you reply to any of them.
2. **The Inside Joke Hoarder** – Only sends memes referencing one conversation you had 4 months ago.
3. **The Thirsty Tagger** – Tags you in flirty content so he can feel like he's "making a move" without actually risking anything.
4. **The Disappearing Comedian** – Sends a meme, gets a laugh, then ghosts until the next one.

Here's the thing:

Memes should be seasoning, not the whole meal. They can't replace real conversation, vulnerability, or effort. If the only time you hear from him is when a trending cat video drops, he's not building a connection he's building a playlist of excuses to never actually connect.

8. "We're Just Vibing" and Other Red Flags Dressed as Chill

Ah yes, *"we're just vibing."* The universal code for *I'm enjoying your company but have zero plans to define this or take it anywhere serious.*

It sounds relaxed, effortless, cool. And that's exactly why it's dangerous, because "chill" can become the perfect camouflage for commitment-phobia.

Why "just vibing" feels good at first:

- It's low-pressure.
- It keeps things fun and flirty.

- You convince yourself you're being "modern" and "free-spirited."

Why it's actually a red flag:

- It's commitment limbo.
- It leaves you emotionally invested without security.
- It gives him an easy exit when he's bored: "I thought we were just vibing."

Translation Guide:

- "Let's not label it yet" = I want the perks without the responsibilities.
- "We don't need to plan ahead" = I'm keeping my calendar open for better options.
- "We're just seeing where it goes" = I already know where it's not going.

The Reality Check:

There's a difference between keeping things light because it's new and keeping things vague because it suits their agenda.

If you're craving clarity and he's serving vibes only, you're not being "chill"; you're being kept on ice.

9. He Says He's "Not Ready" but Wants to Cuddle? Sir.

Oh, he's *not ready* for a relationship... but somehow, he's ready to lay in your bed, wrap himself around you, and breathe on your neck like a Victorian widower in mourning? Interesting.

This is the emotional equivalent of "I'm not hungry" and then eating half your fries.

Why they do it:

- Physical closeness without emotional accountability feels safe *for them*.
- They get the comfort of a relationship without having to commit to one.

- They know affection is addictive, and they're happy to give you just enough to keep you hooked.

Red Flag Checklist:

- Wants cuddles but won't discuss the future.
- Initiates intimacy only when it's convenient for them.
- Gets weirdly defensive if you ask what this means.
- Calls you "babe" during snuggles, then "friend" in daylight.

The Truth Bomb:

If someone tells you they're "not ready," believe them, but also believe the part they're not saying: *I'm not ready for you.*

You deserve affection that comes with clarity, not confusion.

If you let him play *boyfriend* at night and *single guy* by day, you're not building a connection you're running a very comfortable daycare for grown men.

10. Is He Healing or Hiding? A Guide to the Emotionally Unavailable

Some men are genuinely healing. Others are just hiding behind the word like it's an emotional invisibility cloak. The trick is figuring out which one you've got before you invest your heart and half your sanity.

Signs He's Actually Healing:

- He's actively working on himself (therapy, journaling, healthy habits).
- He communicates his limits clearly and respectfully.
- He sets boundaries *and* respects yours.
- You see slow but steady progress in how he shows up for you.

Signs He's Hiding:

- Talks about "needing to work on himself" but makes zero changes.
- Uses his past as a hall pass for bad behaviour.
- Disappears when emotions get too real, reappears when he's bored.
- Wants your emotional labour without offering emotional safety.

Why This Matters:

When someone's genuinely healing, the pace might be slower, but there's direction. When they're hiding, there's just circles.

One will eventually meet you at the table. The other will keep you in the waiting room until you're emotionally dehydrated.

Your Power Move:

If his actions don't match his healing talk, don't stand there holding the tissues and cheering him on. Let him do the work *without* making you collateral damage in the process.

11. The "I'm Not Like Other Guys" Starter Pack

When a man says, *"I'm not like other guys,"* what he usually means is, *I'm exactly like other guys, but I have a Spotify playlist and one unusual hobby.*

This line is often the bait for women who've been burned before. It promises safety, depth, and individuality. But more often than not, it's the equivalent of slapping "organic" on a packet of Oreos, nice branding, same product inside.

Starter Pack Contents:

- At least one "deep" photo on his dating profile (reading a book, staring at a sunset, holding a dog).
- An obscure band T-shirt he wears like a personality trait.
- Vague spiritual or philosophical quotes sprinkled into conversation.
- The line "I just see the world differently" followed by... not seeing your needs at all.

The Red Flag Twist:

If he has to tell you he's different, chances are he's not. The men who are truly unlike the rest show it through their actions, respect, honesty, and consistency, not through a slogan.

Your Power Move:

When someone claims they're "not like other guys," don't be impressed by the words. Watch for proof. Because a man who's truly different will never need to convince you, you'll just know.

12. Sweet Talk & Vanishing Acts – Welcome to the Crumb Parade

If you've ever had a man shower you with sweet words one day, then disappear like he got abducted by aliens the next, congratulations, you've met a proud member of the **Crumb Parade**.

The Crumb Parade isn't about grand gestures. It's about doing *just enough* to keep you around without ever giving you the real thing.

Common Parade Floats:

- **The Compliment Cannon** – Fires "You're so beautiful" texts into your inbox, then ghosts before you can even reply.
- **The Weekend Wonder** – Gives you 48 hours of attention, then nothing until the next Friday night.
- **The Hope Dealer** – Talks about all the things you'll "do someday" but somehow never picks a date.
- **The Smoke Bomb** – Disappears right after an intimate moment, leaving you replaying the conversation like it's a crime scene investigation.

Why it's so confusing:

Sweet talk lights up your brain like a pinball machine. It makes you feel chosen, desired, and special. But when it's followed by a vanishing act, you're left chasing that feeling like it's the last train out of town.

The Truth Bomb:

A man who genuinely values you doesn't vanish. He stays. And you don't have to beg for consistency; it's built into who he is.

13. How to Spot Breadcrumbs Before the First Date

Breadcrumbing doesn't magically start after you meet; most of the time, the clues are baked right into your early conversations. You just have to know what to look for.

Pre-Date Breadcrumb Clues:

- **Minimal Effort Messaging** – Replies like "lol" or "nice" that make you wonder if he's texting from a coma.
- **The Perpetual Planner** – Talks about meeting up but never locks in a day or time.

- **The Peak-and-Disappear** – Sends a burst of flirty messages, then vanishes for days.
- **The Copy-Paste Compliments** – Generic lines that feel like they've been sent to 14 other women that morning.
- **The No-Question Club** – Never asks about *you* but will happily monologue about himself.

Bonus Clues from His Profile:

- Vague captions like "Here for a good time, not a long time."
- Photos with ex-cropped arms still in the shot.
- Every bio sentence ends with a winky face.

Why this matters:

If he can't show consistent interest before the first date, that's not going to magically change afterwards. Dating is like house hunting; if it's already showing cracks in the foundation, don't buy it, hoping the roof will fix itself.

14. Red Flags Disguised as Spontaneous Road Trips

A last-minute road trip can *sound* romantic - adventure, playlists, roadside snacks. But in the wrong hands, it's less "The Notebook" and more "unpaid Uber driver with emotional labour."

Why it can be a trap:

Spontaneous trips create an illusion of intimacy. You're stuck in a small space for hours, sharing music and laughter, and it feels like connection. But often, it's a distraction from the fact that he's not offering you anything real in day-to-day life.

The Tell-Tale Signs It's a Red Flag Trip:

- There's no actual plan; you're "just going to see where the road takes us." Translation: *I haven't thought this through, and I'm hoping you won't notice.*
- The main destination benefits him (picking up something for his place, visiting his mate, running errands).
- He "forgets" to book accommodation, turning it into an excuse to crash at a friend's place… or yours.
- You're footing the bill for fuel, food, or both.

Why it works on you (for a while):

Road trips feel cinematic. They have built-in photo ops, private moments, and the promise of a story you can tell later. But remember, if the only big effort he's made for you is a trip that's convenient for him, it's not romance, it's logistics.

The Rule:

A real spontaneous trip is fun *and* thoughtful. A fake one is just another breadcrumb in a bigger trail of half-effort.

15. The Chase Game (And Why It's Designed to Drain You)

Some men don't want a relationship; they want the *thrill* of the chase. The second they catch you? Game over.

The chase game isn't about love, respect, or connection. It's about ego. They enjoy the pursuit because it makes them feel powerful, desirable, and in control. Once they "win" you, the dopamine fades, and so does their effort.

How the Chase Game Works:

1. **The Hook** – Over-the-top attention to get you intrigued.
2. **The Sprint** – Constant texts, plans, compliments, he's everywhere.
3. **The Catch** – You start to reciprocate.
4. **The Fade** – He slows down, leaving you wondering what you did wrong.
5. **The Reset** – Disappears until you pull away… then starts the chase all over again.

Why It's So Exhausting:

- You're stuck in a constant loop of proving your worth.
- Your self-esteem starts depending on his attention.
- The relationship becomes about keeping him interested instead of asking if *you* are.

Your Power Move:

Step out of the race. The right man won't need to be entertained to stay interested; he'll be invested from the start, and that interest will *grow*, not fade.

16. I Don't Think He's Busy, Babe - I Think He's Boring

We've all been there, convincing ourselves that his lack of effort is because he's "just so busy right now." But let's be honest: people make time for what matters to them. If weeks go by without plans, calls, or meaningful conversation, he's not swamped... he's just not showing up.

Busy vs. Boring:

- **Busy** people still check in, even briefly.
- **Boring** people only surface when they're lonely, bored, or need something.
- **Busy** people tell you what's going on and make future plans.
- **Boring** people leave you guessing if they even remember your last date.

The Hard Truth:

Sometimes "busy" is code for "I'm not prioritising you," and dressing it up with the word busy makes it sound less cruel. But if every conversation feels like pulling teeth and every date takes a miracle to arrange, you're not in a rom-com… you're in a slow, energy-draining sitcom without the laugh track.

Your Reminder:

You are not auditioning to be someone's part-time entertainment. The right person won't need convincing to fit you into their life, they'll be excited to.

PART TWO:

Crumb Connoisseurs Anonymous

16. How to Rewire Your Heart So You Stop Craving Crumbs

When you've been living on crumbs long enough, a stale, half-hearted "hey" can feel like a gourmet meal. That's not romance, that's malnutrition.

Why We Crave Crumbs:

- Our brains get addicted to the unpredictable dopamine hits.
- We've been conditioned to mistake *attention* for *affection*.
- The little bits feel precious because they're rare, and rare things feel valuable.

The Rewire Process:

1. **Admit You're Hungry** – No more pretending you're "fine" with scraps. Name it: you want the full meal.
2. **Change the Recipe** – Start noticing the difference between genuine care and half-effort.
3. **Go Cold Turkey** – No "just one last text" or "maybe he'll change." Detox means *cutting it off completely.*
4. **Feed Yourself First** – Fill your life with things and people that give you consistent nourishment: hobbies, friendships, routines that make you feel good.
5. **Raise Your Standards** – Crumbs stop being tempting when you've tasted the real thing.

The Truth:

A man who really wants to be with you won't keep you guessing. Your job is to train your heart to see crumbs for what they are: proof you're wasting your appetite on the wrong table.

17. What Your Brain Thinks Breadcrumbs Mean (It's Wrong)

Your brain is a drama queen. Give it a crumb, a text, a like, a late-night "miss you", and it lights up like a Christmas tree. The problem? It's confusing *attention* with *affection* and *novelty* with *value*.

The Science-y Bit (In Plain English):

- Every crumb is a tiny dopamine hit. Dopamine = "Ooh, this feels good, give me more."
- Intermittent rewards (a crumb here, nothing for days, then another crumb) are the fastest way to create an addiction.
- Your brain starts chasing the *high* instead of questioning the *source*.

The Reality Check:

Your brain doesn't care if the person is actually good for you; it just cares that the pattern feels familiar. And if you grew up with inconsistent love or attention? Boom. It feels like home, even if "home" was chaos.

The Fix:

- **Pause before reacting** – Ask: "Is this contact meaningful or just convenient for them?"
- **Break the pattern** – Stop rewarding crumbs with your energy.
- **Teach your brain new rules** – Fill it with consistent, healthy connections so the erratic ones lose their shine.

Remember:

Your brain might *think* crumbs mean "he cares." But in reality, they mean "he knows exactly how little he can give you before you walk away."

18. But We Had a Vibe – Trauma, Fantasy, and Misread Energy

Ah, *the vibe*. That intoxicating rush when you click with someone instantly. You talk for hours, laugh at the same weird memes, and finish each other's... unhealthy attachment sentences. It feels like destiny, but sometimes, that "destiny" is just your trauma and his avoidance holding hands.

Why the Vibe Feels So Strong:

- Your nervous system recognises the emotional chaos as "familiar."
- Fantasy fills in the blanks, you decide he's perfect before you have actual evidence.

- You mistake chemistry for compatibility (spoiler: they're not the same).

The Dangerous Part:

When the vibe is that strong, you ignore the slow replies, the mixed signals, and the way you always leave interactions feeling… unsettled. You tell yourself, *But we had a connection*. No, babe, you had a *moment*. Moments are not relationships.

The Reality Check:

A true connection doesn't confuse you, drain you, or make you question your worth. That "vibe" might actually be a spark from emotional friction, and friction burns out fast.

Your Power Move:

Before you crown someone "soulmate," ask: *Was this a vibe or was it a vision board I built in my head after one good conversation?*

19. Did I Fall or Was I Pushed? The Illusion of Connection

Sometimes it feels like you "fell" for someone, but if you replay the tape, you'll see they were giving you a carefully curated highlight reel designed to tip you headfirst. That wasn't fate. That was a push.

How the Push Works:

- **Fast-Tracked Intimacy** – Deep conversations on night one, but somehow you still don't know his middle name.
- **Targeted Attention** – He zeros in on your insecurities and makes you feel seen… then uses it as leverage later.

- **Mirror Effect** – He reflects your values, hobbies, and goals back to you, so you feel perfectly matched.
- **Selective Vulnerability** – Shares just enough personal detail to hook you, but never enough to risk actual emotional intimacy.

Why It Feels Like Falling:

Your brain loves a shortcut. This kind of intensity feels like skipping the awkward "getting to know you" stage. It feels safe, familiar, and electric. But the speed isn't about connection, it's about control.

The Truth Bomb:

If someone engineered the "fall" with a perfectly timed push, you weren't swept off your feet; you were placed exactly where they wanted you. Real connection grows. Manufactured connection manipulates.

20. Girl Math – If He Texted You After 3 Days, Is That Love?

Welcome to Girl Math: the emotional algebra we do to turn bare-minimum behaviour into romantic proof.

He took three days to text back? Obviously, he was just *building suspense*.

He liked your Instagram post but didn't reply to your message? That's basically a *digital love letter*.

The Classic Girl Math Formulas:

- (Delayed Reply × Heart Emoji) ÷ Your Loneliness = He's Thinking of Me
- (Three Memes + One Compliment) − Any Actual Plans = He's Serious About Us
- (Sudden "U up?" + No Context) × 2 a.m. = He Misses Me

Why We Do It:

Our brains want closure and meaning, even if we have to invent it. So, we stretch the numbers, fudge the equations, and round up until a crumb looks like a feast.

The Problem:

When you keep recalculating the math to justify his actions, you're inflating his value while bankrupting your own.

Your Power Move:

Stop being the accountant of his attention. If the numbers don't add up without mental gymnastics, it's not love, it's bad math.

21. The Almost Relationship and Its Emotional Hangover

The almost relationship is sneaky. It looks like a relationship, feels like a relationship, but somehow... it never *was* one.

You did the dates, the late-night talks, the sleepovers. You met his friends, maybe even his dog. But there was no label, no clarity, and no commitment, just a lot of *"Let's not ruin what we have"*. Spoiler: what you had was a situationship in fancy wrapping.

Why It Hurts So Much:

- You invested real feelings into something without stability.

- You grieved a future that technically never existed.
- You feel foolish for missing someone who was never truly yours.

The Emotional Hangover Symptoms:

- Overanalysing every conversation, looking for where it "went wrong."
- Cringing at memories you once replayed for comfort.
- Random waves of sadness that hit like bad tequila the morning after.

The Truth:

You don't need to minimise your pain just because it "wasn't official." Almost relationships can break your heart just as much, sometimes more, because you never got the closure that comes with a clear ending.

Your Power Move:

Mourn it, learn from it, then raise your standards so "almost" never happens again. The next time, you're not settling for "kinda", you're holding out for *absolutely*.

22. How to Know You're Trauma-Bonded to a Ghost

A trauma bond is already messy. Add ghosting to the mix, and suddenly you're clinging to a connection with someone who isn't even *there*.

What This Looks Like:

- You feel intense loyalty to someone who vanished without warning.

- You replay the good moments like a highlight reel, ignoring the abrupt ending.
- You defend them to friends who are (rightly) telling you to move on.
- You feel like they *could* come back any day... so you don't close the door.

Why It Happens:

- Intermittent reinforcement (aka crumbs) wires your brain to crave their approval even more when it's withheld.
- Your nervous system mistakes anxiety for attraction.
- You're addicted to the idea of "fixing" things and getting that emotional hit again.

Signs You're Bonded to a Ghost:

- You keep their number saved "just in case."
- Every notification makes your heart race.
- You measure new people against an idealised version of them that never actually existed.

The Break:

You can't heal with the door half-open. Delete the number. Block the socials. Let the ghost stay dead. A love story can't exist when one person is only haunting it.

22. How to Know You're Trauma-Bonded to a Ghost

A trauma bond is already messy. Add ghosting to the mix, and suddenly you're clinging to a connection with someone who isn't even *there*.

What This Looks Like:

- You feel intense loyalty to someone who vanished without warning.
- You replay the good moments like a highlight reel, ignoring the abrupt ending.
- You defend them to friends who are (rightly) telling you to move on.
- You feel like they *could* come back any day… so you don't close the door.

Why It Happens:

- Intermittent reinforcement (aka crumbs) wires your brain to crave their approval even more when it's withheld.
- Your nervous system mistakes anxiety for attraction.
- You're addicted to the idea of "fixing" things and getting that emotional hit again.

Signs You're Bonded to a Ghost:

- You keep their number saved "just in case."
- Every notification makes your heart race.
- You measure new people against an idealised version of them that never actually existed.

The Break:

You can't heal with the door half-open. Delete the number. Block the socials. Let the ghost stay dead. A love story can't exist when one person is only haunting it.

23. If You're in His Phone, as Maybe You're Not

If you've ever glanced at his phone and seen your name saved as something vague, "Maybe [Your Name]," "Gym Girl," "Hinge," "???", congratulations, you've just been demoted to a *non-priority contact*.

What It Really Means:

- You're not important enough to warrant your full name.
- He hasn't decided what you are to him (and isn't in a hurry to figure it out).
- You're one of multiple "maybes" in his rotation.

The Emotional Fallout:

It's a subtle signal that you're not secure in his life. And while it might seem small, labels matter, even the ones in a phone contact list.

Your Power Move:

Don't stick around waiting for a contact name upgrade. If he can't even save your name properly, he's not about to prioritise your heart. Change *your* contact list instead, by deleting him.

24. Did He Actually Do Anything Wrong, or Am I Just Starving?

Sometimes the question isn't, *Was he terrible?* It's, *am I so deprived of genuine care that the smallest thing feels monumental?*

He replied to your text within an hour, and you're swooning.

He asked how your day was, and you're planning the wedding seating chart.

He remembered your coffee order once, and you're telling your friends, "He's different."

The Starvation Effect:

When you've been living on emotional crumbs, any small kindness feels huge. But that's not because it's exceptional, it's because you've been underfed for so long.

How to Tell the Difference:

- **Healthy Interest:** Consistent, respectful, and not surprising because it's the norm.
- **Starvation High:** Inconsistent, minimal, and leaves you anxious for the next dose.

The Truth Bomb:

Not every man who treats you "better than the last guy" is good for you; some are just slightly less bad. Don't confuse "less bad" with "good."

Your Power Move:

Stop measuring his worth by the behaviour of your worst ex. Measure it against the standard you *deserve*.

25. You're Not Crazy, He's Just Inconsistent

If you've ever found yourself saying, *"Maybe I'm overreacting,"* let me reassure you, you're not. You're reacting to inconsistency, and inconsistency will make even the most grounded woman feel like she's losing her mind.

Why Inconsistency Messes with You:

- It creates emotional whiplash; one day, you're adored, the next, you're ignored.
- It keeps you guessing, so you put more energy into figuring him out than enjoying the connection.

- It triggers the part of your brain that craves stability, making you work harder for scraps.

The Cycle:

1. He shows up fully, making you feel safe.
2. He pulls away, leaving you confused.
3. You chase the closeness, thinking you did something wrong.
4. He returns, acting like nothing happened.
5. Repeat until your self-worth is running on fumes.

The Truth:

You don't need to decode his mood swings; you need to recognise that he's showing you exactly who he is.

Your Power Move:

Stop trying to solve the puzzle. Healthy relationships don't require detective work; they feel consistent, calm, and secure.

26. The Power of Blocking – Digitally and Emotionally

Blocking isn't petty - it's protection. It's how you reclaim your mental space from someone who's been squatting in it rent-free.

Why Digital Blocking Works:

- Removes temptation to "just check" what they're up to.
- Stops their crumbs from popping up in your feed at 2 a.m. when your guard is down.
- Sends a clear message: *access denied*.

Why Emotional Blocking Matters Even More:

- You stop replaying the good parts like a highlight reel.
- You stop fantasising about them "finally getting it together."
- You close the door on "what if" and open the door to "what's next."

The Pushback Myth:

Some people will say blocking is dramatic. Those people have never experienced the mental drain of leaving the door cracked open for someone who shouldn't be in your life at all.

Your Power Move:

Block. Mute. Delete. Whatever it takes to cut the feed. Because sometimes the most loving thing you can do for yourself is to make sure the line stays dead.

27. Inner Child Needs a Snack, Not a Crumb Man

When you keep falling for crumb men, it's not just your adult self-making the choice; it's often your inner child, still hoping to finally get the attention she deserved years ago.

Why This Happens:

- Childhood wounds around love and attention set your "normal" at inconsistent care.
- Crumb men mimic that pattern, so it feels familiar, even if it's unhealthy.
- Your inner child thinks, *If I can make him love me, maybe it means I was always lovable.*

The Problem:

You can't heal your inner child by giving her the same diet that hurt her in the first place. Crumbs won't fill her up; they'll just keep her hungry.

The Snack Upgrade:

- **Feed Her Consistency:** Surround yourself with people who show up.
- **Feed Her Joy:** Hobbies, experiences, and self-care that make you feel alive.
- **Feed Her Safety:** Environments where you don't have to prove your worth to be accepted.

Your Power Move:

When your inner child cries out for love, don't hand her a crumb, man, hand her a snack. Something nourishing, real, and sustaining. Love that feeds you doesn't leave you starving.

28. You Don't Want Him, You Want Closure

Let's be real, half the time you think you "want him back," you don't actually want *him*. You want the missing pieces filled in, the "why" explained, and the ending wrapped in something that makes sense.

Why We Confuse the Two:

- The brain craves resolution more than it craves truth.
- Rejection triggers the need to *prove* we were worth choosing.
- It's easier to chase the familiar than face the uncertainty of moving on.

The Problem with Chasing Closure from Him:

- People who left without clarity rarely come back with honesty.
- Even if they explain, it usually won't feel "good enough."
- You give them more power by making them the gatekeeper of your healing.

The Truth:

Closure is an inside job. It's not about what they say, it's about what you decide. You don't need their blessing to move forward.

Your Power Move:

Stop framing it as unfinished business with him. Finish it yourself.

You're not craving his love, babe, you're craving the peace that comes from letting go.

29. When You Romanticise Red Flags and Call It Chemistry

You know that rush you feel when you meet someone and your heart races, your palms sweat, and you feel like you've known them forever? Yeah... sometimes that's not *chemistry*. Sometimes it's your nervous system recognising chaos and saying, *Oh, hey, old friend.*

How We Dress Up Red Flags as Romance:

- Mistaking unpredictability for excitement.
- Calling emotional unavailability "mysterious."

- Interpreting mixed signals as "he's just complicated."
- Convincing ourselves the arguments mean "we're passionate."

Why We Do It:

- We've been taught love should feel dramatic to be real.
- Familiar patterns (even unhealthy ones) feel safe.
- Movies and TV have sold us the "enemies to lovers" trope without the therapy bill.

The Truth Bomb:

That spark you're feeling? It might be adrenaline, not affection. And adrenaline is great for roller coasters, but terrible for relationships.

Your Power Move:

Next time you feel that instant, magnetic pull, ask yourself: *Is this attraction... or am I romanticising a walking red flag because it feels like a plot twist?*

30. He's Not Deep, He's Just Avoidant with a Spotify Playlist

Some women meet a guy who shares moody playlists, quotes obscure authors, and stares out the window like he's brooding over the meaning of life… and immediately think, *Wow, he's so deep.*

But here's the truth: sometimes he's not deep, he's just emotionally avoidant with good curation skills.

Why It Feels Profound:

- He talks about art, music, and philosophy, but never his feelings.

- He sends you songs instead of communicating directly.
- He's mysterious, but only because you have no actual data on who he is.

The Avoidance Disguise:

- Shares lyrics instead of truths.
- Uses "I'm just a private person" to dodge intimacy.
- Makes you work to "decode" him, which keeps you distracted from the fact he's not showing up.

The Reality:

Depth is measured by vulnerability, not vinyl collections. A man can know every Radiohead lyric and still have the emotional range of a teaspoon.

Your Power Move:

Stop falling for the aesthetic of depth. If he can't have an honest, open conversation about his feelings, his Spotify Wrapped is just a well-decorated wall between you and the truth.

PART THREE: Red Flags, Replays & Reckonings

The hilarious, horrifying catalogue of what we've all dated.

31. Red Flags Disguised as Spontaneous Road Trips

Ah, yes, the romantic getaway that turns out to be a logistical nightmare in disguise. You thought it was *The Notebook*. It was actually *Fast & Furious: The Errands Edition*.

The Setup:

- "Pack a bag, babe, I'm surprising you."
- You imagine wineries, sunsets, and scenic hikes.
- You end up driving three hours to help him pick up a second-hand fridge off Marketplace.

The Reality:

- No booked accommodation.
- Snacks? Just whatever he found at the servo.
- "Sightseeing" is actually watching him chat to his mate about car parts.

Why It's a Red Flag:

Spontaneity is fun when it's paired with effort. But if the only time he makes big moves is when it's convenient for *him*, you're not on a romantic adventure; you're just his co-pilot in the laziness parade.

32. He's Just Bad at Texting and Other Lies I Told Myself

Ah, the classic excuse: *"He's just bad at texting."*

No, babe. He's just bad at prioritising you.

The Mental Gymnastics:

- "Maybe he's busy." (He posted three Instagram Stories.)
- "Maybe he's not a phone person." (Somehow manages to send memes to his mates.)
- "Maybe he prefers in-person communication." (Cancels plans. Again.)

Why We Say It:

Because admitting he's simply *not interested enough* is painful. It's easier to believe he's a sweet, analogue soul who just can't figure out the little keyboard than face the fact that you're not a priority.

The Truth Bomb:

Men run multinational companies from their phones. They run side hustles, group chats, and fantasy football leagues, all while sending their mates play-by-play updates. If he wanted to text you, he would.

Your Power Move:

Stop grading him on a curve. "Bad at texting" is not a personality trait; it's a communication choice.

33. Do You Like Him or Just the Way He Held That Coffee?

Sometimes it's not love, it's latte lust. He picked up his coffee with that casual confidence, smiled just right, maybe rolled up his sleeves... and suddenly you're imagining your future children's names.

The Bare-Minimum Spark:

- The way he said "flat white" like he owned the café.
- The little smirk when he stirred his sugar.
- That one moment, he looked at you over the cup like it was a slow-burn romance movie.

Why This Happens:

Our brains are wired to romanticise tiny gestures, especially when we're starved for genuine connection. It's easier to fixate on the *aesthetic* than check if there's any actual substance.

The Reality Check:

The way he holds a coffee cup tells you… that he can hold a coffee cup. That's it. It doesn't tell you if he's emotionally available, kind, or capable of showing up for you consistently.

Your Power Move:

Enjoy the view, but don't build a love story on latte art. The right man will hold your coffee *and* hold you through life's chaos.

34. He Calls You Babe but Forgets Your Birthday

He's got no trouble remembering to call you *babe* in texts, in person, even mid-argument… but when your birthday rolls around? Crickets.

The Babe Effect:

- "Babe" is easy. It's generic, low-effort, and requires zero memory.
- It keeps the vibe affectionate without committing to actual thoughtfulness.
- It's basically verbal filler dressed up as intimacy.

Why It Stings:

Birthdays are personal. They're the one day a year that's entirely about you. Forgetting it says, "I'm here for the easy stuff, but don't expect me to show up when it matters."

The Truth Bomb:

If he can remember the stats from his fantasy football league, his mate's dog's name, and the exact time his favourite bar opens... he can remember your birthday. He just didn't.

Your Power Move:

Don't be dazzled by pet names if there's no real care behind them. The right man won't just call you babe; he'll remember *the day you were born* without Facebook having to remind him.

35. The Guy Who Cries During Sex and Disappears by Morning

At first, it feels like a deeply intimate moment, you're connecting, the energy's intense, and then... tears. Not the happy kind. Not the *oh wow, this is so beautiful* kind. The *there's a story here and I'm not ready for it* kind.

The Experience:

- You pause, concerned, asking, "Are you okay?"
- He says, "I just... I've never felt this close to someone."
- You go into emotional support mode, thinking you've unlocked a tender, vulnerable soul.

- By morning, he's gone. No text. No note. No explanation.

Why This Happens:

- The tears were about something else entirely, an ex, unresolved trauma, or the crushing realisation he can't actually handle intimacy.
- Vulnerability scared him, so instead of processing it, he bolted.
- Some men confuse sexual connection with emotional safety, and when the high fades, so does their presence.

The Truth:

It's not your job to fix, heal, or decode someone who emotionally ejects at sunrise. You're a person, not a pit stop on his healing journey.

Your Power Move:

Don't romanticise the tears. Vulnerability means nothing without consistency.

36. Men Who Do Yoga and Still Ghost You

You thought dating a man who does yoga meant he'd be grounded, mindful, and emotionally evolved. Instead, he can hold crow pose for two minutes but can't hold a conversation about where this relationship is going.

The Yoga Man Fantasy:

- You imagine peaceful Sunday mornings, doing sun salutations together.
- He talks about "being present" and "opening the heart chakra."
- He wears linen pants and quotes Rumi on Instagram.

The Reality:

- Disappears for days without explanation.
- Uses "I needed to realign my energy" as an excuse for not texting back.
- Treats communication like it's a competitive sport in which silence is a winning move.

The Truth Bomb:

Flexibility on the mat doesn't always mean flexibility in relationships. A man can chant "namaste" and still leave you on read.

Your Power Move:

Stop assuming hobbies equal character. The right man's consistency will be in his actions, not just in his downward dog.

37. The Guy with an Audi and No Emotional Depth

He pulls up in a sleek Audi, the paint gleaming, music perfectly cued. He smells like a department store cologne counter. You think, *Wow, he's got his life together.* Spoiler: he doesn't.

The Audi Illusion:

- The car is clean, but his communication is a mess.
- He spends more on detailing than on actual dates.
- He's mastered acceleration but brakes hard when emotions come up.

Why It's Misleading:

Material polish can disguise emotional poverty. The car is a symbol of control, success, and status, all things he wants you to see, but under the hood, there's no depth, no vulnerability, no consistent care.

The Truth Bomb:

An Audi can get you from point A to point B. It cannot get you to emotional intimacy.

Your Power Move:

Don't confuse horsepower with heart power. The right man's emotional depth won't need chrome to shine.

38. He Had Crystals and a Co-Star App, But Still Breadcrumbed Me

You thought dating a man who charged his crystals under the moon and checked his Co-Star astrology app daily meant he'd be spiritually in tune. Instead, he's spiritually performative and emotionally unavailable.

The Crystal Courtship:

- He talks about "aligning energies" while aligning himself with three other women.
- Sends you screenshots of your astrology compatibility but never commits to actual plans.

- Owns a rose quartz "for love" but uses it as a paperweight for unpaid bills.

Why It's Confusing:

Spiritual language can sound like emotional depth. "Mercury retrograde messed with my communication" feels better than "I didn't prioritise texting you back."

The Truth Bomb:

Crystals don't fix character. You can sage a man's apartment, but you can't sage away his avoidance issues.

Your Power Move:

Judge him on his consistency, not his crystal collection. A real spiritual man will ground himself in truth, not just in moonlight rituals.

39. I'm Just Focusing on Me (While Actively Leading You On)

Ah, the classic line: *"I'm just focusing on me right now."* Sounds mature. Sounds self-aware. But somehow, he's still texting you late at night, still flirting, still planting little seeds of "maybe one day."

The Mixed Message Menu:

- Talks about how he "isn't ready for a relationship" while behaving exactly like a boyfriend when it suits him.
- Keeps you emotionally invested just enough so you don't move on.
- Drops breadcrumbs of hope between long stretches of silence.

Why It's Manipulative:

He's creating a safety net. You're the backup plan, the comfort zone, the person he knows will be there when he's "done focusing on himself."

The Truth Bomb:

If he were truly focusing on himself, he wouldn't need you orbiting around his ego to keep him entertained.

Your Power Move:

When someone says they're focusing on themselves, let them, without you as their emotional side hustle.

40. The Man Who Asked for My Netflix Password Mid-Breakup

There's a special place in the Hall of Red Flags for the man who, in the middle of ending things, pauses to say, *"Hey, before I go... can I still use your Netflix?"*

The Scene:

- You're emotional, maybe crying.
- He's explaining why "it's not you, it's him."
- Then, out of nowhere, he's negotiating access to your streaming services like it's part of the settlement.

Why It's So Telling:

- Shows zero awareness of how inappropriate the timing is.
- Reveals that he's still thinking about his convenience, even in the breakup moment.
- Proves that your relationship was transactional in more ways than one.

The Truth Bomb:

If someone can treat your heartbreak as an opportunity to secure a login, they were never emotionally invested in the first place.

Your Power Move:

Change the password before the door even closes behind him.

41. Why He's Obsessed with You but Still Not Dating You

He watches all your stories. He remembers tiny details you told him months ago. He texts you out of the blue just to say he was thinking about you... And yet, somehow, you are still not his girlfriend.

The Confusing Combo:

- **High Attention** – Constant interaction, inside jokes, and late-night conversations.
- **Low Action** – No concrete plans, no labels, no actual progression.
- **High Emotion** – Talks like you're already together.

- **Low Commitment** – Lives like he's single.

Why He Does It:

- He likes the ego boost of your attention.
- You're his emotional safety net, not his romantic priority.
- He's keeping you on the hook while leaving his options open.

The Truth Bomb:

If a man is obsessed with you but refuses to date you, it's not because he's scared of how much he feels. It's because he likes the comfort without the responsibility.

Your Power Move:

Stop confusing obsession with devotion. The right man won't just orbit you; he'll stand beside you.

42. The Spiritual One Who Said He Was Processing for 7 Months

He spoke in soft tones, burned sage, and claimed to be "deeply connected to his higher self." But when it came to committing to you? He was *processing*. For seven. Whole. Months.

The Processing Excuse:

- "I just need to align my energy first."
- "The universe is telling me to slow down."
- "I'm doing shadow work... so I can't really be in a relationship right now."

Why It's a Red Flag:

- Spiritual language doesn't replace emotional maturity.
- "Processing" becomes a get-out-of-effort-free card.
- It keeps you in limbo while making him sound wise instead of avoidant.

The Truth Bomb:

Healing is real. But if someone's processing for months without making any actual moves toward you, they're not preparing to love you, they're preparing to let you down gently… eventually.

Your Power Move:

Wish him luck on his journey, then take yourself out of his waiting room.

43. The Guy Who Gave You a Nickname but Not a Label

He calls you "baby," "sweetheart," or some cutesy nickname only he uses. It makes you feel special… until you realise that's all he's offering you.

The Nickname Trap:

- Nicknames create intimacy without commitment.
- They give the *illusion* of a bond while keeping things undefined.
- They make you feel claimed without actually being chosen.

Why He Does It:

- It softens the blow of not calling you, his girlfriend.
- It keeps you emotionally attached without having to step up.
- It's a tool to keep you close when he senses you pulling away.

The Truth Bomb:

A man who wants you will give you a label *and* a nickname. One without the other is just a placeholder for someone he doesn't want to lose but doesn't want to fully claim.

Your Power Move:

If he can name you but can't name the relationship, stop answering to anything but your own worth.

44. He Said He Missed Me… Then Replied 8 Days Later

He sends *"I miss you"* like it's a grand romantic gesture. You feel a little flutter… until you notice he's been MIA for over a week.

The Timeline Problem:

- Day 1: "I miss you."
- Days 2–8: Radio silence.
- Day 9: Acts like nothing happened.

Why It's Manipulative:

- It gives you a dopamine hit without any follow-up action.

- It's bait to keep you emotionally hooked.
- It shifts the focus from his absence to your reaction.

The Truth Bomb:

If he really missed you, you wouldn't be counting days between texts. Missing someone is a feeling. Acting on it is a choice.

Your Power Move:

Stop accepting declarations with no delivery. "I miss you" without effort is just a pretty lie with bad timing.

45. If You Think He Might Be in a Situationship, You Are

Situationships are like quicksand, you don't realise you're in one until you're already knee-deep and sinking.

The Giveaway Signs:

- You're doing all the relationship things without the relationship title.
- Conversations about the future feel like you're asking for his Netflix password.
- You're not sure if you can post a photo together without it being "too much."

Why We Pretend It's Not One:

- Admitting it forces you to acknowledge he's not all in.
- You cling to the hope that "it's just taking time."
- You don't want to start over, so you settle for the almost.

The Truth Bomb:

If you're even asking yourself, *"Is this a situationship?"* It is. Certainty feels like certainty. Confusion is your answer.

Your Power Move:

Stop waiting for him to promote you. If he's not choosing you fully, choose yourself instead.

PART FOUR: Escape Plans & Glow-Ups

How to stop the cycle and get your damn life back.

46. Getting the Hell Out Without Texting "U up?" First

It's over. You know it's over. But then, at 11:47 p.m., your phone glows and your brain whispers, *Just one more…*

The Late-Night Lies We Tell Ourselves:

- "It's just to see how he's doing." (It's not.)
- "I'll feel better if I get answers." (You won't.)
- "Maybe he's changed." (He hasn't.)

Why You Have to Resist:

- Every "U up?" resets your healing clock to zero.
- You teach him you're still available, no matter the disrespect.
- You give crumbs another shot at becoming a meal, they won't.

The Truth Bomb:

You're not going to get closure at midnight in a text thread that's 80% memes and 20% "wyd?". You're going to get a brief dopamine hit followed by emotional food poisoning.

Your Power Move:

Delete the number before your thumbs betray you. If you must be up at midnight, text your group chat, order dessert, or rewatch a comfort show, but don't text him.

47. Don't Block to Get a Reaction, Block to Get Peace

Blocking isn't about proving a point. It's about ending the noise. If you do it to get a dramatic response, you're still centring him. If you do it for your own peace, you're centring *you*.

Why Blocking for a Reaction Backfires:

- You'll end up checking to see if he noticed.
- If he doesn't react, you'll feel worse.
- If he does react, you risk getting pulled back in.

Why Blocking for Peace Works:

- No more random messages yanking you back into old emotions.
- You remove the temptation to stalk his socials.
- Your nervous system finally gets to rest.

The Truth Bomb:

Blocking is not petty, dramatic, or "immature." It's a boundary with a digital lock.

Your Power Move:

When you block, do it quietly. No announcement, no warning, no last-word text. Just reclaim your peace and go live a life he can't watch anymore.

48. The Breakup Is the Closure

You don't need his essay-length explanation. You don't need a final dinner, a long walk, or one last "talk" that turns into another three months of half-relationship. The breakup *is* the closure.

Why We Chase Extra Closure:

- We think if we understand "why," it'll hurt less.
- We want to change their mind.
- We confuse confusion with hope.

The Reality:

Closure isn't something they give you; it's something you decide. Waiting for them to deliver it keeps you tied to the exact person you're trying to let go of.

The Truth Bomb:

If they ended it, that *was* the reason. If they drifted away, that *was* the explanation. Anything else is just extra words to soften the blow, and sometimes, they won't even give you that.

Your Power Move:

Accept the ending as the answer. Then, write your own period on the story instead of letting them keep it open-ended.

49. A Glow-Up Isn't Just Lip Gloss, It's Self-Respect

A true glow-up isn't just hotter selfies and a new haircut, it's an inside job. Because while looking good is satisfying, *feeling good* is where the real power kicks in.

The Surface Glow-Up:

- New makeup routine.
- Gym membership.
- Outfit upgrades.
- Instagram captions that say *"thriving"* but still low-key hope he's watching.

The Real Glow-Up:

- Boundaries so strong they could survive a Category 5 ex.
- No longer feeling the urge to check his socials.
- Choosing yourself every single time.
- Living a life you're proud of, even if no one's watching.

The Truth Bomb:

Anyone can buy lip gloss. Not everyone can rebuild their self-worth from the ground up.

Your Power Move:

Glow from the inside out, not so he notices, but so *you* can't help but notice how far you've come.

50. Delete the Chat, Not Just the Contact

Deleting his number is a start, but if you're keeping the chat history, you're basically leaving the emotional door wide open.

Why the Chat Has to Go:

- You'll scroll back "just to check" and end up re-reading every sweet word like it's evidence in a trial.
- Old conversations will tempt you to rewrite the ending in your head.
- Seeing his name in your chat list is like keeping an open tab at a bar you swore you'd never drink at again.

The Truth Bomb:

You can't heal while re-reading your own heartbreak. Those texts aren't proof of love; they're proof of how much you settled for.

Your Power Move:

Hit delete. No backups, no screenshots, no "just in case." The only history worth keeping is the one you're building without him.

51. You're Not Too Sensitive, You're Just Finally Listening to Yourself

For years, people may have told you to "lighten up" or "stop overreacting." But here's the truth: you weren't too sensitive; you were ignoring your own boundaries to keep other people comfortable.

Why It Feels Like Sensitivity:

- You're noticing disrespect earlier than you used to.
- Things you once let slide now feel intolerable.
- You're reacting to micro-cracks before they turn into chasms.

The Shift:

When you raise your standards, what you once tolerated will suddenly feel unbearable. That's not a weakness, that's self-awareness.

The Truth Bomb:

People who benefited from your silence will call you sensitive the moment you speak up.

Your Power Move:

Listen to your instincts. If something feels off, it probably is. Sensitivity isn't a flaw; it's an alarm system. And yours is finally switched on.

52. Stop Texting Him. He's a Crumb

Every time you text him first, you're giving him exactly what he wants, your attention, without his effort.

Why You Keep Doing It:

- You want answers.
- You hope this time will be different.
- You confuse persistence with romance.

The Problem:

Each message you send teaches him that he doesn't have to pursue you, because you'll always do the work for him.

The Truth Bomb:

You're not being "chill" or "low maintenance." You're being breadcrumbed, and you're helping him bake the loaf.

Your Power Move:

Put the phone down. If he wants to talk to you, let him do the reaching out. And if he doesn't? That's your answer; no response *is* a response.

53. You Can't Heal Where You're Being Hurt

You can't fix your self-worth in the same place it was broken. Staying in a relationship that's draining you and calling it "working on things" is like trying to recover from food poisoning by eating the same dodgy takeaway.

Why We Stay:

- We want the pain to turn into proof we were right to try.
- We hope they'll change if we just love them harder.
- We mistake endurance for strength.

The Hard Truth:

Healing requires safety. And if you're constantly anxious, second-guessing yourself, or waiting for the next let-down, you're not healing, you're surviving.

Your Power Move:

Step away from the source of the pain. The right environment will let you breathe, rebuild, and remember what it's like to feel good again.

54. If He Wanted To, He Would (And He Hasn't Babe)

This one's simple. Men who want to see you, see you. Men who want to call you, call you. Men who want to commit, commit. Anything else is noise.

Why We Complicate It:

- We romanticise struggle.
- We buy into excuses because the alternative hurts.
- We cling to "potential" instead of reality.

The Truth Bomb:

Effort is not ambiguous. When someone truly wants to be with you, you won't have to decode mixed signals or read between the lines; the message will be loud, clear, and consistent.

Your Power Move:

Stop making exceptions for him and start making standards for yourself. If he hasn't, he doesn't want to, and that's all you need to know.

55. Don't Let the Memes Fool You. That's Not Communication

He sends you TikTok's, Instagram reels, and memes that make you laugh. Cute. But if that's 90% of your "conversations," babe, you're not talking, you're just swapping content.

Why It Feels Like Connection:

- Shared humour makes you feel close.
- You assume if he's thinking of you when he sees a meme, he must care.
- It creates tiny dopamine hits without the effort of a real exchange.

The Problem:

Memes can't replace meaningful conversations about your feelings, boundaries, or where the relationship is heading. You can't build intimacy out of punchlines.

The Truth Bomb:

If he can send you a meme but can't ask how your day was, he's not communicating; he's entertaining himself.

Your Power Move:

Enjoy the memes but expect more. Real connection comes from words that aren't recycled from the internet.

56. Let Them Miss You from the Block List

If someone lost access to you, that's the consequence. You don't unblock so they can "realise what they had", you let them figure that out in silence.

Why This Works:

- Absence makes them notice the loss.
- You remove the temptation for them to breadcrumb you back in.
- You protect your peace while they deal with their regret (or don't).

The Truth Bomb:

The block list isn't a timeout. It's a permanent VIP list for people who no longer get to sit at your table.

Your Power Move:

Stay blocked, stay unbothered, and let them learn that your absence is the price of their behaviour.

57. You Can Be Horny and Have Boundaries

Yes, you can want sex and still want respect. Your libido is not a permission slip for someone to treat you like an afterthought.

The Myth:

If you're sexually attracted to someone, you have to ignore red flags to get what you want.

Wrong. You can be turned on and still turn *them* down.

Why Boundaries Matter More When You're Tempted:

- Lust can blur logic, but boundaries bring it back into focus.
- You protect your emotional wellbeing along with your physical health.
- You show yourself you can have both pleasure and standards.

The Truth Bomb:

Saying yes to your desires doesn't mean saying yes to someone who's inconsistent, disrespectful, or just plain wrong for you.

Your Power Move:

Decide what you want *and* what you won't tolerate, and don't let hormones negotiate on your behalf.

58. Heal So You Don't Write Him into Your Next Story

If you don't take the time to heal, he'll sneak into your next chapter disguised as a "different" man. Same energy, new packaging.

Why This Happens:

- Unresolved wounds keep attracting familiar patterns.
- You mistake comfort for compatibility.
- You write new love stories with the same old plot twists.

The Problem:

Healing isn't just about moving on; it's about reprogramming your taste, so you don't crave what hurt you.

The Truth Bomb:

You can't rewrite your love life if you're still using him as a reference point for romance.

Your Power Move:

Do the inner work. Heal, grow, and learn so thoroughly that he wouldn't even recognise the woman you've become, and she wouldn't recognise him as an option.

59. You're Not a Mystery to Be Solved, you're a Standard to Be Met

You are not a puzzle for someone to piece together at their convenience. You are the whole picture, and not everyone gets to hang it on their wall.

The Problem with Being "Mysterious":

- It invites people who chase the thrill of discovery, not the work of commitment.
- It makes your worth feel like something to be *earned* instead of respected from the start.
- It attracts men who love the challenge but disappear once they think they've "figured you out."

The Truth:

You are not meant to be decoded. You are meant to be valued. And your value doesn't come from being "different" or "hard to read", it comes from knowing who you are and what you deserve.

Your Power Move:

Stop letting people treat you like a riddle. You're not here to be solved, you're here to be met at your level.

60. From Feral to Fabulous – A Post-Crumb Comeback Plan

You've been through the emotional trenches, the late-night tears, the overthinking marathons, the "just one more text" relapses. Now it's time to rise from the ashes like a phoenix... in better shoes.

Step 1: De-Crumb Your Life

- Block, delete, and unfollow.
- Purge his hoodie from your wardrobe (yes, even if it's comfy).
- Replace the sad playlists with "main character" energy bangers.

Step 2: Build Your Glow-Up Routine

- Daily rituals that make you feel strong, centred, and unstoppable.
- Reconnect with friends and hobbies you neglected.
- Treat yourself like you're dating *you*.

Step 3: Upgrade Your Standards

- Write down your new non-negotiables.
- Commit to catching red flags at the *pink* stage.
- Stop letting boredom, loneliness, or lust pick your partners.

The Truth Bomb:

Your comeback isn't about proving anything to him; it's about proving to *yourself* that you were always the prize.

Your Power Move:

Walk into your next chapter so fabulous that crumbs don't even register on your menu anymore.

PART FIVE: The Gingerbread Men Archives

*Real stories, funny disasters, and holy-sh*t-he-really-said-that moments. *

61. The Time He Sent Me a Playlist Instead of Apologising

We'd argued, not a small spat, but the kind where you expect at least a phone call, maybe flowers, maybe him showing up at your door ready to grovel. Instead... I get a Spotify link.

The Playlist Apology Experience:

- Title: *Sorry, Babe* (already suspicious).
- Track one: "I'm Sorry" by whoever.
- Track two: "Let's Get It On."
- Track three: a random Ed Sheeran song about love that in no way matched the context of why I was upset.

The Problem:

A playlist is cute for a crush, not for fixing an emotional betrayal. Music doesn't replace accountability. I don't need your curated vibes, I need your actual words.

The Truth Bomb:

If you can't say "I was wrong" without hiding behind song lyrics, you're not apologising. You're just outsourcing your feelings to Spotify.

Your Power Move:

Next time, I'll make my own playlist. First track? "Irreplaceable" by Beyoncé.

62. A Man Gave Me a Rock. Not a Ring. Just… A Rock

He said he had a "special gift" for me. My mind went to jewellery, a keepsake, maybe something sentimental. He opened his hand… and it was literally a rock. From the ground.

The Presentation:

- No box.
- No story.
- Just, "I thought of you when I saw it."

The Problem:

A gift should say, "I know you." This said, "I was outside."

The Truth Bomb:

If a man gives you something you could have picked up in your own driveway, he's not gifting, he's littering with confidence.

Your Power Move:

Keep the rock. Use it as a paperweight for all the standards you've now raised.

63. I Asked What We Were, and He Said I Thought We Were Vibes

We'd been seeing each other for months, dates, sleepovers, meeting each other's friends. One night, I finally asked, *"So… what are we?"*

He smiled like he was about to drop the most romantic line of my life and said,

"I thought we were… vibes."

The Translation:

- "I enjoy your company but have zero plans to define it."

- "I want relationship benefits without the label."
- "Please don't ask me for anything that requires effort."

Why It's Infuriating:

Vibes are for beach days and playlists, not for building an actual connection.

The Truth Bomb:

If you're "just vibes," you're also just temporary.

Your Power Move:

Thank him for clarifying and then go find someone who's more than a feeling.

64. I'm Not Emotionally Ready While Planning Our Future Vacay

One week, he's booking flights for a romantic getaway. The next, he's telling you he's "not emotionally ready for a relationship." Sir, which is it, are we sipping cocktails in Bali or am I crying in my kitchen?

The Mixed Signal Olympics:

- Talks about "our future" but won't commit to the present.
- Plans a trip like a boyfriend but acts single as soon as you're back home.
- Says you're "moving too fast" while sending you hotel links.

Why It's a Mind Game:

- Keeps you invested with big gestures that don't match his emotional availability.
- Gives him an easy out: "I never promised anything."

The Truth Bomb:

If someone's willing to plan months ahead for a holiday but not for a relationship, they're not building a life with you; they're booking an experience for themselves.

Your Power Move:

Next time, go on the trip. Just change the name on the ticket to someone who's actually all in.

65. He Asked Me to Babysit His Dog, Then Dated Someone Else

He said he was "too busy to hang out" because of work. Then he asked me to watch his dog for the weekend. Of course, I said yes, because I love dogs and, apparently, ignoring red flags.

While I was walking his golden retriever and refilling the water bowl, he was... on a date. With someone else. I know because she posted their dinner on Instagram.

Why It Stings:

- I was caring for something he loves while he was out entertaining someone he *might*.
- It made me realise he trusted me with his dog more than he valued me as a partner.

The Truth Bomb:

If a man uses you as free pet care while pursuing other women, he's not just disrespectful, he's outsourcing his responsibilities while dodging his own emotional mess.

Your Power Move:

Love the dog. Leave the man.

66. My Crumb Man Said I Was Too Empowered

In the middle of an argument about, you guessed it, his lack of effort, he actually said, *"You're just... too empowered."*

Translation:

- "You don't let me get away with doing the bare minimum."
- "I can't manipulate you like I'm used to."
- "I miss the days when women didn't call me out."

Why It's Ridiculous:

Empowerment is not a flaw. But to a man who thrives on control, it's a threat.

The Truth Bomb:

If your confidence, boundaries, and standards are "too much," it's because they're too much for *him*. Not for the right person.

Your Power Move:

Wear "too empowered" like a badge of honour, preferably while walking out the door he thought you'd never leave.

67. I Found Out I Was the Side Quest

For months, I thought I was the main storyline, the heroine, the love interest, the plot twist he couldn't live without. Turns out, I was just... the side quest.

How I Found Out:

- Our "big plans" always got bumped for other "priorities."
- I never met the main characters in his life, friends, family, anyone permanent.
- When we weren't together, I might as well have been erased from his world.

The Side Quest Signs:

- You're exciting, but not essential.
- He invests just enough to keep you in the game, but never enough to reach the next level.
- You're a detour, not a destination.

The Truth Bomb:

If you're not part of his main storyline, you're not the one he's building the future around.

Your Power Move:

Drop out of his game entirely. Go find someone where you *are* the plot.

68. We Matched Dated Ghosted Matched Again

It started like every dating app success story: cute banter, great first date, promises of more. Then, poof. Ghosted. Weeks later, there he was... matching with me *again*.

The Repeat Offender Pattern:

- Acts like the first ghosting never happened.
- Sends the same opening line he used the first time.
- Pretends the emotional Houdini act was "just bad timing."

Why They Do It:

- Short-term memory for their own bad behaviour.
- Fishing to see if the door's still open.
- Banking on your curiosity (or boredom) to give them another shot.

The Truth Bomb:

If he disappeared once without explanation, he'll do it again. Matching twice doesn't make him fate; it makes him a slow learner.

Your Power Move:

Swipe left on reruns. You've already seen how this episode ends.

69. He Took Me to IKEA and Never Spoke Again

It felt like a milestone, walking through IKEA together, pointing at couches, debating which fake plants we'd *hypothetically* own. We shared meatballs. We laughed in the lighting section. I thought, *Wow, this is getting serious.*

Then... nothing. No calls. No texts. It was like we'd never debated flatware in aisle 14.

Why It Stung:

- IKEA is the unofficial couples' test; it felt like he was inviting me into future territory.

- We'd basically "played house" for an afternoon.
- It's hard to be ghosted when you're still emotionally attached to a bookshelf you never bought.

The Truth Bomb:

If a man can pick out throw pillows with you and then vanish, he wasn't building a home; he was killing an afternoon.

Your Power Move:

Buy the couch yourself. Sit on it knowing you dodged a lifetime of him.

70. The One Who Said You're Like a Sister to Me After Sex

We'd just been intimate, the kind of intimate where you think, *Well, this definitely confirms we're into each other.* I was still catching my breath when he looked at me and said, *"You're like a sister to me."*

Why That's... A Lot:

- Incest-adjacent vibes are never sexy.
- It instantly killed any post-romantic glow.
- It made me question every interaction we'd ever had.

Possible Explanations (Non-Good):

- He panicked and said the first thing that came to mind.
- He thought it was a compliment (it wasn't).
- He's emotionally tangled in ways I do not have the qualifications to untangle.

The Truth Bomb:

If someone compares you to a family member in the afterglow, the relationship is already over, you just need to leave the room to make it official.

Your Power Move:

Add this one to the list of things therapy will unpack later.

71. I Met His Family Before I Met His Commitment

It seemed like a big step, meeting his family. His mum hugged me, his dad offered me a beer, his sister asked about my job. I left thinking, *Wow, he must be serious about me.*

Turns out, I wasn't the only "special guest" they'd met that month.

Why It's Misleading:

- Meeting the family feels like a relationship milestone, but for some men, it's just casual socialising with a side of ego boost.

- He gets to look like a committed guy without actually committing.
- You get emotionally invested in a man who just likes showing off that he's dating someone attractive and fun.

The Truth Bomb:

Family introductions mean nothing if they're not backed by consistent action toward building a future with you.

Your Power Move:

Next time you meet the family, make sure you've also met the commitment; otherwise, it's just a meet-and-greet with no sequel.

72. He Complimented My Boundaries Then Crossed Every One

On our second date, he said, *"I love how you have boundaries. It's so attractive when a woman knows her worth."* I thought, *finally, a man who gets it.*

Fast-forward a few weeks, and he'd:

- Pushed past timelines I'd set for intimacy.
- Tried to guilt me into plans I'd said no to.
- Treated my "no" as "convince me harder."

Why It's Manipulative:

- Complimenting your boundaries early creates the illusion of respect.
- Crossing them later relies on the hope you won't notice or won't want to ruin the "good thing" you thought you had.

The Truth Bomb:

A man who truly respects your boundaries doesn't just admire them; he upholds them, even when it's inconvenient for him.

Your Power Move:

If he praises your boundaries and then breaks them, praise yourself for walking away.

73. The Date Who Cried About His Ex Then Asked for Nudes

We were halfway through dinner when he started tearing up about his ex. I did the compassionate thing, listened, offered tissues, reassured him.

By dessert, the tears had dried. On the walk to my car, he leaned in and said, *"So… you wanna send me something sexy later?"*

Why It's Wild:

- Emotional vulnerability can be genuine… until it's just a prelude to manipulation.

- Switching from heartbreak to horniness in under an hour is not a "mood shift"; it's a red flag in motion.
- It cheapens the trust you offered in that moment.

The Truth Bomb:

A man who uses his sadness as a shortcut to intimacy isn't looking for connection; he's looking for distraction.

Your Power Move:

Save your compassion for someone who won't treat it like foreplay.

74. I Thought It Was a Relationship. He Thought It Was Thursday

We were doing all the relationship things, weekly date nights, sleepovers, meeting each other's friends. I was in deep. So, when I brought up "us," he looked genuinely confused and said,

"Wait... you thought this was, like... a thing?"

Translation:

- All the effort he put in was for convenience, not commitment.
- He was fine with the situation as long as no one mentioned labels.

- To him, our time together was just… something to do.

Why It Hurts:

- You feel like you imagined the entire connection.
- You start second-guessing every moment you thought was special.
- It's not just rejection; it's a reality check with a side of humiliation.

The Truth Bomb:

If someone's actions look like a relationship but they say it's not one, believe the words, not the fantasy.

Your Power Move:

Don't waste Thursdays, or any day, on someone who doesn't see you as more than a time slot.

75. We Should See Other People, Bro, I Haven't Seen You

After weeks of cancelled plans, unanswered texts, and the kind of "relationship" that existed more in theory than in reality, he finally said,

"I think we should see other people."

Sir... we haven't even seen *each other*.

Why It's Ridiculous:

- He's breaking up with an arrangement that barely existed.

- It's framed like a difficult, noble decision when it's actually just stating the obvious.
- It implies exclusivity that was never there to begin with.

The Truth Bomb:

Some men will end things just to feel like they were in something worth ending.

Your Power Move:

Respond with, *"Sure, I've been doing that already."* And mean it.

PART SIX:
Love Without Crumbs

What healthy actually looks like and how to stop settling for snack-size romance.

76. What Real Commitment Actually Feels Like

Real commitment doesn't feel like chasing. It doesn't feel like waiting for a text that may or may not come or wondering if the weekend plans will stick this time.

It feels steady. Reliable. Calm. It's knowing where you stand without having to decode messages, run mental gymnastics, or lower your standards.

What It Looks Like:

- He follows through on what he says.
- You don't have to question if you're a priority, you feel like one.

- Disagreements don't turn into disappearing acts.
- You both choose each other daily, without being prompted.

The Truth Bomb:

Commitment isn't a grand gesture once a month; it's the small, consistent actions every day that build trust and security.

Your Power Move:

If you're still feeling anxious in a committed relationship, ask yourself: *Is this real commitment… or just crumbs dressed up as one?*

77. How to Spot the Green Flags Before You Miss Them

When you've been trained to scan for red flags, healthy love can feel… suspicious. You're so used to chaos that calm feels like boredom, and consistency feels like a trick.

Green Flags to Look For:

- **Clear Communication** – He tells you where you stand without making you guess.
- **Keeps His Word** – If he says he'll call, he calls. If he says he'll be there, he shows up.
- **Respect for Boundaries** – Doesn't push, test, or try to negotiate your limits.

- **Conflict Without Punishment** – You can disagree without silent treatment or retaliation.
- **Mutual Effort** – The relationship doesn't rely on you holding it together.

Why We Miss Them:

- Green flags don't spike adrenaline the way red flags do.
- Healthy behaviour feels unfamiliar if you've only known inconsistency.

The Truth Bomb:

Spotting red flags keeps you safe. Spotting green flags helps you grow. You need both skills to build something real.

Your Power Move:

When you see a green flag, don't brush it off; lean in. That's where love gets good.

78. Trust Isn't Earned Through Vibes, It's Built Through Action

Good vibes are nice. They make for a fun first date, a great playlist, and a good laugh over drinks. But they don't build trust.

How Trust Is Actually Built:

- Showing up when they say they will.
- Following through on promises, even when it's inconvenient.
- Consistency over time, not intensity in the beginning.
- Choosing honesty over the easy out.

Why Vibes Aren't Enough:

- Vibes are instant. Trust takes time.
- Anyone can create a feeling, not everyone can back it with proof.
- You can't build a relationship on mood lighting and "we just click."

The Truth Bomb:

Trust isn't about how you feel around someone on a good day, it's about how they treat you on the hard days.

Your Power Move:

If someone's words and actions don't match, stop trusting the vibes and start trusting the evidence.

78. Trust Isn't Earned Through Vibes, It's Built Through Action

Good vibes are nice. They make for a fun first date, a great playlist, and a good laugh over drinks. But they don't build trust.

How Trust Is Actually Built:

- Showing up when they say they will.
- Following through on promises, even when it's inconvenient.
- Consistency over time, not intensity in the beginning.
- Choosing honesty over the easy out.

Why Vibes Aren't Enough:

- Vibes are instant. Trust takes time.
- Anyone can create a feeling, not everyone can back it with proof.
- You can't build a relationship on mood lighting and "we just click."

The Truth Bomb:

Trust isn't about how you feel around someone on a good day; it's about how they treat you on the hard days.

Your Power Move:

If someone's words and actions don't match, stop trusting the vibes and start trusting the evidence.

79. He Texts Back, He Shows Up, That's It. That's The Standard

Healthy relationships aren't built on games, suspense, or "Will he? Won't he?" moments. They're built on the boring, beautiful basics: he replies, he follows through, he's there.

Why We Overcomplicate It:

- We've been trained to think love has to be dramatic to be real.
- We mistake inconsistency for passion.
- We've normalised chasing as part of the "fun."

What Meeting the Standard Looks Like:

- He answers your messages in a reasonable time.
- He follows through on plans without last-minute chaos.
- He doesn't disappear and then reappear like he's in a sitcom.

The Truth Bomb:

If a man can't manage the bare minimum, communication and presence, he's not your partner; he's a distraction.

Your Power Move:

Stop celebrating crumbs as commitment. If he texts back and shows up, that's not "special", that's the baseline.

80. No Mixed Signals, No Crumbs, Just Consistency

Real love isn't a guessing game. You don't spend nights wondering what a text meant or why he suddenly went quiet. You don't get highs followed by crushing lows. You get stability.

What Consistency Looks Like:

- His words match his actions.
- His interest doesn't fluctuate with his mood or convenience.
- You feel secure even when you're not together.

Why It Matters:

Consistency isn't boring, it's freedom. It frees you from overthinking, analysing, and constantly checking your worth against his attention.

The Truth Bomb:

Mixed signals are just red flags with good PR. Crumbs are just proof he doesn't have a full meal to give you.

Your Power Move:

Make consistency the entry requirement. Anything less is an automatic no.

81. Love Shouldn't Feel Like a Mystery Novel

You shouldn't need to be a detective to figure out if someone cares about you. Love isn't meant to be a plot twist or a cliffhanger; it's meant to be clear.

When Love Starts Feeling Like a Mystery:

- You're decoding texts like they're written in Morse code.
- You're piecing together scraps of information to guess where you stand.
- You feel like you're constantly one conversation away from "figuring it out."

Why This Is a Problem:

Mystery keeps you hooked but not fulfilled. It feeds the chase, not the connection.

The Truth Bomb:

Love shouldn't be a suspense story with you as the main character who's also the only one trying to solve the case.

Your Power Move:

If it's not clear, it's not love. The right person won't keep you guessing; they'll make sure you know.

82. Don't Romanticise Confusion, That's Not Love

Confusion isn't passion. Mixed signals aren't depth. And hot-and-cold behaviour isn't "complicated love", it's just inconsistency with a side of drama.

Why We Mistake Confusion for Love:

- Movies and TV glamorise the "will they/won't they" dynamic.
- The emotional highs and lows mimic adrenaline, which feels exciting.
- We've been taught that love should be hard work, so we tolerate chaos.

The Reality:

Love isn't supposed to feel like a constant emotional puzzle. It should feel steady, safe, and easy to read.

The Truth Bomb:

If you're constantly trying to interpret his actions, you're not in love; you're in limbo.

Your Power Move:

Save the drama for Netflix. In your love life, choose clarity over confusion every time.

83. Healthy Love Is Boring at First, And That's Hot

At first, healthy love might feel... quiet. No drama. No adrenaline rush from mixed signals. Just steady, predictable care. And if you've been raised on chaos? That calm can feel almost suspicious.

Why It's Actually Sexy:

- You're not losing sleep over unanswered texts.
- You're not riding emotional rollercoasters; you're on a scenic train ride with snacks.
- The focus is on building something real, not chasing temporary highs.

What "Boring" Really Means:

- Consistent communication.
- Respect for your time and boundaries.
- Emotional safety without having to earn it.

The Truth Bomb:

Boring is only boring if you're addicted to chaos. Once you heal, boring becomes the hottest thing you've ever experienced.

Your Power Move:

Reframe boring as dependable, trustworthy, and secure, because that's where the real intimacy lives.

84. You Don't Have to Heal to Be Loved, You Just Have to Be Safe

There's a popular lie that you must be *fully healed* before anyone can love you. Here's the truth: you don't need to be perfect, you just need to be in a safe, supportive relationship where your healing can happen.

Why This Matters:

- Waiting until you're "done healing" is like waiting until you're in perfect shape to join a gym.
- Healing is a lifelong process; you'll always be evolving.
- The right relationship can actually help you grow faster by providing stability.

What Safety Looks Like in Love:

- You can express your needs without fear.
- Your vulnerabilities are met with care, not criticism.
- Disagreements don't threaten the relationship.

The Truth Bomb:

Healing isn't a prerequisite for love, but safety is.

Your Power Move:

Stop delaying your happiness until you're "ready." Focus on finding someone who treats your healing as sacred, not as a burden.

85. Rewrite Your Fantasy to Match Your Future

Sometimes the fantasy in your head is the biggest red flag in the relationship. You picture the future version of them, the one who changes, shows up, and loves you the way you need, while the real version in front of you is still serving crumbs.

Why This Keeps You Stuck:

- You're in love with potential, not reality.
- You excuse bad behaviour because of what *might* happen someday.
- You pour energy into building a dream that only exists in your head.

The Shift You Need:

Instead of asking, "What could this be?" ask, "What is this *now*?" Then rewrite your love story based on what supports the life you actually want.

Signs Your Fantasy Needs an Edit:

- You're constantly defending them to yourself or your friends.
- The relationship exists more in your imagination than in real life.
- Your needs are "on hold" until they become who you want them to be.

Your Power Move:

Write a new ending where you don't wait for someone to catch up to your worth. Your future deserves a co-star who's already showing up in the role, not one you're still auditioning.

86. Let Them Go So the Right One Can Knock

Sometimes the only thing standing between you and the love you deserve is the person you're scared to release. You keep the door cracked for someone who's already shown they can't, or won't, meet your needs, and in doing so, you're blocking the person who would.

Why We Hold On:

- You're afraid no one else will love you the same way (spoiler: good).
- You're addicted to the crumbs and chaos because it feels familiar.
- Letting go feels like admitting you wasted time.

What Letting Go Really Means:

- You're clearing emotional space.
- You're setting a standard for how you expect to be treated.
- You're trusting that love isn't scarce, but your peace is priceless.

Your Power Move:

Don't just close the door, lock it, seal it, and install a glitter-covered "Do Not Enter" sign. Then open the window for someone better to find you.

87. You Are Not Too Much, You've Just Outgrown Crumbs

They'll call you "too much" when what they really mean is, *"I can't keep up with the level you require."* That's not a flaw. That's proof you've evolved past the stage where bare minimum felt like love.

Why "Too Much" Is a Compliment:

- It means you have standards they can't meet.
- It means you're not shrinking to fit into their comfort zone.
- It means you're operating on a level that filters out the wrong ones.

Outgrowing Crumbs Looks Like:

- You no longer get excited over inconsistent texts.
- You'd rather be single than entertained by chaos.
- You see through "good enough" and politely send it back.

Your Power Move:

Wear your "too much" like a luxury label. If they can't handle your sparkle, they can step aside for someone who can.

88. Love Will Feel Like Coming Home, Not Like Being Tested

Healthy love doesn't keep you guessing. It doesn't make you feel like you're in a never-ending audition, waiting to see if you get the part. Real love feels like walking into a room where you can breathe again.

Signs You've Found "Home" Love:

- You're not constantly measuring your words or timing your replies.
- They don't withhold affection to make you chase it.
- Your worst days don't scare them away.

Why It Feels Different:

- There's no scoreboard, no "you owe me" energy.
- You can be yourself without fear of being "too much" or "not enough."
- Conflict isn't a threat, it's a conversation.

Your Power Move:

Stop chasing the ones who make you feel like you're on trial. Love that feels like home won't test your worth; it will recognise it instantly.

89. You Don't Need Closure, You Need Distance

We chase closure like it's the magic key to finally moving on, but most of the time, what we really want is for them to admit they were wrong and beg us to stay. Spoiler: that's not closure, that's fantasy.

Why Closure Is Overrated:

- It's often just another conversation for them to twist the truth.
- It keeps you in their orbit longer than necessary.
- It turns healing into a group project when it's actually a solo mission.

Why Distance Works Better:

- Distance gives you clarity they never will.
- Silence becomes your answer.
- It lets the craving fade so the logic can take over.

Your Power Move:

Stop waiting for a perfect goodbye. Block. Delete. Create space. You'll be shocked at how much "closure" you find when they no longer have a direct line to you.

90. The Happily Ever After You Wrote for Them? Write It for You

You had a whole romantic epic mapped out in your head, the trips you'd take, the way you'd grow together, the shared couch blanket on Sunday mornings. But here's the twist: you can take every single thing from that vision board and make it yours.

Why This Shift Changes Everything:

- You stop handing someone else the pen to write your story.
- You reclaim all the love and energy you were saving for "someday."
- You become the main character again, not a sidekick in his plot.

How to Do It:

- Swap "we will" for "I will."
- Buy the tickets, book the trip, start the class - without waiting for a plus-one.
- Fill your days with people and things that actually show up.

The Payoff:

The life you thought you needed a partner for? You'll realise you're capable of building it solo. And when someone worthy comes along, they'll be stepping into a story that's already thriving.

PART SEVEN: In the Thick of It – Bite-Sized-Shorts - Truths for Women Stuck in the Almost

For every woman knee-deep in the mess, still trying to convince herself she's not imagining it.

91. How to Set Boundaries Without Sounding Like a TED Talk

- Boundaries don't need a 20-minute PowerPoint presentation. They can be short, sweet, and crystal clear. "That doesn't work for me" is enough. You don't need to prove your worth or defend your reason like you're on trial.

92. Loving Someone Doesn't Mean You Owe Them Access

- Love is not an all-access backstage pass. You can care about someone and still close the door when they're draining your energy. Caring is not the same as self-sacrifice.

93. You're Not Crazy, You're Being Manipulated

- If you're questioning your memory, your feelings, or your sanity every other day, that's not love, that's gaslighting. A healthy man doesn't make you feel like you're losing your mind.

94. How to Say This Isn't Enough and Mean It

- You can say, "This isn't enough for me", and walk away without waiting for him to catch up. If it's not enough now, it won't magically become enough later.

95. If You Have to Beg for the Bare Minimum, It's Not Love

- Love doesn't make you chase basic respect, consistent effort, or honesty. If you have to beg for those, you're in a negotiation, not a relationship.

96. Why You Keep Making Excuses for Him (and How to Stop)

- "He's just busy." "He's going through a lot." "He's not normally like this." These are the little lies we tell ourselves so we can stay. Stop covering for his behaviour and start looking at it.

97. You Can't Change Him with Love. He's Not a Fixer Upper

- You're not HGTV. You can't remodel a man into your dream partner. Love is not a renovation project, if he's not ready, no amount of decorating will make him liveable.

98. When You Want to Leave but Still Hope He'll Get It

- That moment when your bags are packed but you're secretly hoping he runs after you with a grand gesture? Stop waiting for a movie moment. If he doesn't get it now, he won't.

99. You're Not Mean for Having Needs

- Needing affection, attention, or reassurance doesn't make you demanding; it makes you human. A man who makes you feel guilty for having needs is not your person.

100. How to Love Him Without Losing Yourself

- You can give love without emptying your own cup. Keep your hobbies, your friends, and your voice. If you have to shrink to keep him, you'll disappear.

101. You Don't Need to Be Perfect to Deserve Respect

- Respect isn't a reward for flawless behaviour. You can have flaws, bad days, and insecurities and still deserve to be treated with dignity.

102. He Doesn't Have to Hit You to Hurt You

- Abuse isn't always physical. Emotional neglect, manipulation, and constant criticism are just as damaging, sometimes worse.

103. When Apologies Turn into Manipulation

- "I'm sorry, but you…" is not an apology. It's a blame shift. Watch for when "sorry" becomes a weapon instead of a repair.

104. He's Not That Bad Is Not a Justification

- You don't have to wait until he's "that bad" to leave. The absence of extreme abuse doesn't make the relationship good.

105. You Can't Heal in the Same Place That Hurt You

- Trying to heal while staying in a relationship that's breaking you is like trying to put out a fire while standing in the flames.

106. If You Have to Convince Him to Stay, He's Already Gone

- Love is freely given, not persuaded. If you're trying to talk him into staying, you've already lost him, and that's a blessing in disguise.

107. Stop Editing Yourself to Be Easier to Love

- If you're constantly toning yourself down, laughing less, or avoiding topics to "keep the peace," you're in the wrong story.

108. You're Not Dramatic, You're Just Done Being Ignored

- Men love to label women "dramatic" when we've finally stopped tolerating their neglect. It's not drama, it's a wake-up call.

109. How to Set a Boundary Without Apologising After

- "I don't like that" doesn't need a "sorry" tagged on the end. Boundaries are not offences.

110. Save the Screenshot, Not the Relationship

- Keep the receipts for your own clarity but stop trying to use them to win him over. He's not going to suddenly see the light because of a text log, but you might finally see him clearly.

PART EIGHT: The Exit Strategy

When you're ready to leave. What to say, what to expect, and how to survive the suck.

111. How to Break Up Without Making It a Performance

How to keep it short, clear, and free from drama. No "Oscar-worthy" speeches, just honest, grounded exit lines.

Here's the thing about breakups: Hollywood has ruined them for us.

We've been conditioned to believe they need a backdrop of rain, a trembling voice, and a five-minute monologue about fate, growth, and "it's not you, it's me."

Reality check: you are not auditioning for *The Notebook 2: The Bare Minimum Years*.

The healthiest breakups are not performances, they're conversations. And "conversation" in this case means one clear, confident sentence that communicates you're done, without inviting a debate.

Why? Because the longer you talk, the more chances you give him to argue, guilt-trip, or confuse you into staying.

You do not need to convince him you're allowed to leave. You do not need him to understand every reason why. You especially do not need to list every single flaw and hope he finally has a lightbulb moment.

Here's what *not* to do:

- Don't write him a five-paragraph text essay at 2am.
- Don't rehearse a dramatic speech in the mirror for three days straight.
- Don't make it your job to ensure he feels "okay" about the breakup.

Here's what works instead:

- Keep it short: "This relationship isn't working for me anymore."
- Keep it final: "I'm not happy and I need to move on."
- Keep it kind but firm: "I care about you, but this isn't right for me."

Then, and this is the crucial part, stop talking.

If he presses for details, you can say:

- "I've thought a lot about this, and my mind is made up."
- "It's not open for discussion."
- "I need to do what's best for me, and this is it."

Breaking up isn't a group project. You don't need mutual agreement to hand in your decision.

You're not walking away because you hate him; you're walking away because you love yourself more.

The performance is over. The credits are rolling.

Exit stage left, queen.

112. When You Know It's Time Even If It Hurts

That moment when your heart still aches, but your gut is already halfway out the door.

One of the hardest truths to accept is that love isn't always enough.

You can care deeply for someone, miss them before you've even left, and still know with every cell in your body that it's time to go.

This is the part no one tells you about, the grief that comes *before* the goodbye.

It's the quiet knowing that things won't get better, the slow death of your hope, the way your joy feels heavier to carry around him than it does when you're alone.

You start noticing things:

- How much lighter you feel when he's not around.
- How much you edit yourself to avoid his reactions.
- How often you daydream about being anywhere else.

That's not disloyalty. That's your soul trying to get your attention.

We hold on because we're scared of what leaving will feel like. But the truth?

Staying is its own kind of heartbreak.

The slow burn. The endless wait for a version of him who might never show up.

Leaving will hurt. Your body will ache, your heart will protest, and your brain will replay the highlight reel like a cruel sports commentator.

But here's the thing, pain isn't always a sign you're doing the wrong thing.

Sometimes it's a sign you're finally doing the *right* thing.

You can still love someone and choose to walk away.

You can cry over the memories and still decide the future you want doesn't include them.

You can miss them and still never go back.

Because knowing its time isn't about not feeling the pain.

It's about knowing you'll survive it and be better for it.

113. Stop Writing Love Letters to People Who Ghost You

If he disappeared without explanation, he does not need, or deserve, a heartfelt essay from you.

No, he didn't "forget" to text for three weeks. No, he's not "overwhelmed." And no, sending him a beautifully crafted, emotionally vulnerable message will not make him suddenly think, *Wow, she's amazing, I should have treated her better.*

Ghosting is communication. It says, "I don't respect you enough to be honest."

And writing him a love letter in response is like sending a thank-you note to the burglar who stole your wallet.

Here's what happens when you send that long message:

- You hope for closure.
- You get silence.
- You feel worse.

Every time.

Stop telling him how much you care. Stop explaining how hurt you are. Stop giving him the satisfaction of knowing he still has access to your heart.

Instead, write the letter, but don't send it. Burn it, shred it, delete it.

Turn that energy into a note to yourself: *I deserve someone who stays.*

You are not a character in his redemption arc.

If he wanted to keep you, he wouldn't have vanished.

Ghosting is your answer.

Don't waste your ink proving you were worth staying for; go where your words will be read, heard, and valued.

114. The Goodbye Text You Can Actually Copy and Paste

You don't need a TED Talk. You don't need to justify yourself. You just need clarity.

Here's your script:

"Hey, I've realised this isn't the kind of connection I'm looking for. I'm going to step away and focus on what I need. I wish you the best."

That's it. Short. Neutral. Clear.

You are not inviting debate. You are not leaving the door cracked open for "maybe later." You're not giving him homework to improve so he can come back.

Why this works:

- It's respectful without grovelling.
- It avoids blame games that spiral into hours of texts.
- It removes ambiguity so you can stop replaying the conversation in your head.

Send it when you're calm, not at 2 a.m. after three glasses of wine.

Then, mute the chat, put your phone down, and walk away like you're exiting the world's most boring meeting.

You are not available for rebuttals, guilt trips, or romantic plot twists.

You've said what you need to say. The rest is silence and freedom.

115. What to Do When You Miss Him but Still Leave

Missing him doesn't mean you made the wrong choice. It means you're human. You got used to his voice, his routines, the way his name popped up on your phone. Now there's a void, and your brain hates voids.

Here's the truth:

- Missing him is a *feeling*. Going back is an *action*.
- Feelings pass. Actions have consequences.

When you catch yourself wanting to text him, pause and ask: *Will this make me feel better for more than 10 minutes?*

If the answer is no, and it usually is, put the phone down.

Instead:

- Call the friend who always answers on the first ring.
- Write down every reason you left in a note on your phone.
- Go for a walk, even if it's just to the mailbox and back.
- Keep a "Breakup Emergency Kit": chocolate, tea, your favourite movie, and a blanket that feels like a hug.

Here's the mantra:

I can miss him and still move on.

Missing someone is normal. Settling for less than you deserve is optional.

116. Cry Block Repeat — The Breakup Recovery Plan

Grief after a breakup isn't linear. It's a loop - and that loop usually looks like this:

1. Cry.
2. Block.
3. Repeat.

Cry:

Let it out. In the shower, in your car, into a pillow, wherever it hits. You're not weak, you're releasing pressure. Bottling it up will only make it explode in the form of a 2 a.m. "I miss you" text.

Block:

Delete the number, unfollow, unfriend, mute. This is not about being petty; it's about removing the triggers that make you spiral. Healing needs space, and space doesn't exist if his face pops up every time you open your phone.

Repeat:

Some days you'll feel fine. Other days, you'll start the loop over again. That's not failure, that's recovery. Each round gets a little lighter, a little shorter, a little less gut-punching.

If you need a visual, think of it as an emotional laundry cycle. You might have to wash the same shirt a few times before the stain finally fades, but it *will* fade.

The point isn't to never cry.

The point is to cry less over time until one day, you realise you've made it through a whole week without thinking about him.

117. Unfollow His Spotify — Your Healing Needs Silence

Music is a trap. One second, you're cleaning your kitchen, the next you're crying into the dishwasher because *your song* just came on.

Unfollow his playlists. Delete the ones you made together. That "chill Sunday morning" mix is now a landmine of emotional sabotage.

Here's the thing: music imprints on memory. When you hear that track again, your brain drags you back to his couch, his car, his arms. It's not the song making you sad; it's the association.

Replace them.

- Make a "Post-Breakup Power" playlist full of songs you'd never hear with him in the room.
- Find music in genres he hated. (If he despised 80s pop, guess who's now living their best Cyndi Lauper life?)
- Add songs with lyrics that remind you of your own strength, not the size of your loss.

And yes, silence is allowed. Sometimes you don't need background music, you need background *nothing*. The quiet will feel strange at first, but it's in that silence that your mind starts to heal instead of replay.

Unfollow his Spotify. Your heart is not a jukebox for his ghost.

118. Don't Wait for Closure — It Won't Come

Closure is the relationship equivalent of waiting for a package that was never shipped.

You think if you can just get that *one last conversation*, that perfect explanation, you'll finally be able to put it to rest. But the truth? He either doesn't have the answer, or he's never going to give it to you.

Here's why:

- Some people can't face the damage they've caused.
- Some people don't even see it as damage.

- And some… they like knowing you're still wondering.

Closure doesn't come from him, it comes from you deciding *it's done*. You can write your own ending without his signature on it.

Try this instead:

- Write the letter you wish he'd send you and never send it.
- Accept that unanswered questions are still answers.
- Stop re-reading the last text. It's not a prophecy; it's just the last thing he bothered to type.

Closure is not a gift someone hands you. It's a decision you make to stop bleeding for someone who's already walked away.

119. If He Lets You Go, He Never Had You

Real love doesn't just watch you walk away.

If he can let you go without a fight, without reflection, without even trying to meet you halfway, then he never truly *had* you in the first place. He had your time, your attention, your loyalty, but not your heart in the way it deserved to be held.

Someone who truly values you will *show it* when the relationship is on the line. They will reach, they will repair, they will try. If he can shrug and let the door close, it's because he was never invested in keeping it open.

Here's the truth:

- Letting go easily means he wasn't committed.
- You can't lose what was never yours.
- A man who sees your worth doesn't gamble with it.

If he lets you go, don't see it as a rejection; see it as confirmation. He's just freed you to find the one who will hold on with both hands.

120. Leaving Isn't Failure, It's the Start of You

Walking away isn't the end of the story; it's the plot twist where you finally become the main character.

We're taught to see breakups as proof we "couldn't make it work", as if staying in something that was crushing you is the gold standard. It's not. Leaving is not giving up. It's refusing to settle. It's choosing yourself when the relationship stopped choosing you.

Think of it like shedding skin that no longer fits. Yes, it's uncomfortable. Yes, it hurts. But it's also growth. Every ending clears space for the life you actually want, and for the version of you who refuses to take crumbs ever again.

When you leave:

- You reclaim your energy.
- You reset your standards.
- You create room for better love.

Leaving doesn't make you a failure. Staying somewhere that makes you small does.

121. Burn the Fantasies Before They Burn You

One of the hardest parts of leaving isn't losing the man, it's losing the *idea* of him. The fantasy version you built in your head, the one who communicates, remembers your birthday, and doesn't conveniently "forget" you exist when it's inconvenient, feels real. But he's not.

Every time you replay the "good moments," remember: a highlight reel is not the whole movie. That kiss in the rain? Followed by weeks of silence. The deep conversation at 2 a.m.? Followed by him dodging your texts for days.

The fantasy is a liar. It edits out the pain. It lets you hold on to potential instead of reality.

So, here's the truth:

- You don't need to mourn the version of him that never existed.
- You can't date potential.
- You deserve love that's consistent, not conditional.

Let the fantasy go before it burns you alive in the hope of something that was never there.

122. He's Not Your Soulmate, He's Just the Hook Your Wound Caught On

You didn't meet your cosmic twin flame. You met a man who fit perfectly into the cracks your old wounds left behind.

Maybe he mirrored your abandonment issues, so you confused anxiety for attraction. Maybe he gave you just enough attention to feel wanted, but never enough to feel safe, and your brain mistook that push-pull for passion.

The "soulmate" feeling you can't shake? That's not destiny, it's your nervous system mistaking familiarity for love.

He wasn't sent by the universe. He was sent by your unhealed parts, the ones that wanted one more chance to rewrite the story with a different ending. But you can't heal a wound by pressing the same blade into it over and over.

You don't need him to complete you. You were never missing pieces; you just needed to stop letting broken men rearrange you.

123. You Don't Owe a Goodbye to Someone Who Left You Hanging

If he ghosted you, breadcrumbed you, or vanished mid-connection, you don't owe him a neat little bow to wrap things up.

Closure is a two-person job, and he clocked out without notice. That's on him. Your healing is not dependent on his explanation, apology, or sudden reappearance months later with "Hey, stranger."

The truth is, disappearing without a word is its own answer, and it's louder than anything he could have said.

You're allowed to move on without the final scene, the sit-down talk, or the "I just need to get this off my chest" text. Sometimes the healthiest exit is the one where you simply stop walking back to the door he already shut.

124. The First Night Alone: How to Get Through It

The first night alone is the loudest. The silence feels like it has its own heartbeat, and every shadow in your room looks like his ghost.

This is not the night to be a hero.

It's the night to pull out your comfiest blanket, your most indulgent snacks, and the trashiest reality TV you can find. Bonus points if it has a reunion episode; nothing bonds you to strangers faster than watching them air their mess.

Turn your phone on "Do Not Disturb" if you can. If you can't, move it across the room so you're less likely to check his socials on reflex.

Cry if you need to. Laugh at stupid memes if you can. Keep the lights soft and your expectations lower. The only goal tonight is to make it to morning without texting him.

Because the first night without him isn't the start of your loneliness, it's the start of getting yourself back.

125. Grief Is Normal, Obsession Is a Symptom

Grief is the wave that knocks you over after you leave someone. It's the ache in your chest, the lump in your throat, the tears you don't even try to stop. That's normal. It's proof you cared.

Obsession is different. Obsession is refreshing his Instagram every hour. Reading old texts until your eyes sting. Replaying arguments in your head like you're going to find the "gotcha" moment that wins him back.

Grief honours what you lost. Obsession chains you to it.

It's okay to miss him. It's not okay to make missing him your full-time job. Let the grief come and go like weather, but don't let obsession build a house in your head.

If you find yourself slipping into obsession, interrupt it. Call a friend. Leave the house. Play music that has nothing to do with him. Train your brain to crave something else.

Because the day will come when your grief fades, but if you've been feeding obsession, it will still be sitting there, hungry for more of you.

126. Keep the Memories, Leave the Man

Not every memory is a warning sign. Some are sunsets, laughter in a kitchen, or the way he once made you feel safe. You don't have to erase them to move on.

But here's the thing, you can keep a memory without keeping the man. You can acknowledge that a moment was beautiful and still know the relationship was wrong.

Memories are snapshots. They are not a contract to stay. You are allowed to frame the good ones in your mind without re-inviting the person who created them back into your life.

Because the truth is, the man in the memory and the man you left are not always the same. One existed for a moment. The other is who you actually had to live with.

Honour the moments. Let go of the person.

127. You Can Be the One That Got Away and Stay Away

There's a dangerous romance in the idea of being *the one that got away.*

It sounds poetic, like you're a bittersweet song he'll play on repeat when the new girl isn't looking.

And maybe you are. Maybe one day, he'll scroll through old photos, sigh dramatically, and wonder what could have been. That's fine. Let him.

But here's the secret, you don't have to *go back* to keep that title.

You can be the one who got away... and stayed away.

Because "getting away" isn't about making him regret losing you. It's about reclaiming yourself so fully that there's no version of events where you'd ever go back.

You're not a chapter he gets to re-read. You're the book he should have finished when he had the chance.

128. How to Stop Checking if He's Seen Your Story

You post something, a cute selfie, a cryptic lyric, maybe a shot of you looking suspiciously happy, and then it begins.

The refresh.

The scroll.

The desperate little dopamine hit when his name shows up in the viewers' list.

Here's the truth: that list is not a love letter. It's not proof he cares. It's an *algorithm*. People watch stories for the same reason they click on random TikToks: curiosity, boredom, and muscle memory.

Every time you check if he's seen it, you're handing him space in your head rent-free. And babe, we're in a housing crisis.

The fix? Post it, log off, and live like you're the one worth watching, because you are.

Let him wonder if you're thinking about him. Spoiler: you're not.

129. The Block List Vision Board Method

Blocking isn't petty, it's personal policy.

Think of your block list as a velvet rope, and you're the bouncer at the VIP lounge of your peace. Not everyone gets in, especially not the man who made "seen" his love language.

Here's the twist: your block list isn't just about removing people; it's about *reminding yourself who you're becoming*. Every name you add is a little declaration:

- "I'm not tolerating less than I deserve."
- "I'm choosing quiet over chaos."

- "I'm building something they don't get to watch."

If you're feeling dramatic (and honestly, why not?), screenshot your block list and save it in a folder called *Proof I Love Myself*. Print it out. Frame it. Hang it above your desk.

Your future self will thank you and she'll have no idea what their username even was.

130. Loving Him Was a Season, not a Sentence

Some loves are meant to change you, not keep you.

They come like summer storms, intense, beautiful, impossible to hold. And when they pass, you don't stand in the rain begging them to stay. You dry off. You grow.

Loving him was a chapter, not your whole story. A season, not a life sentence. You are not chained to the memories, the what-ifs, or the version of you who kept hoping he'd rise to meet you.

Seasons teach. Seasons end.

And when they do, you get to plant something new in the space he left behind. Something that blooms for *you* this time

PART NINE:

Healing & Becoming Her

131. You Don't Need Him to Become Her

Becoming *her*, the woman who knows her worth, speaks her truth, and builds her life unapologetically, doesn't require his love, his approval, or his presence.

You don't need him to inspire your glow-up, your boundaries, or your joy.

You become *her* the moment you decide you're done living on crumbs.

The moment you stop waiting for someone to choose you and start choosing yourself.

The version of you that you're becoming isn't built on him.

She's built on you, and that's why she's unshakable.

132. You Were Always the Magic. He Was Just the Plot Twist

You didn't become magical when he showed up, and you didn't stop being magical when he left.

He was a chapter, not the whole book.

He may have been the spark, the plot twist, the unexpected page-turner,

But *you* were the story all along.

The way you love, the way you laugh, the way you rise, that's the real magic.

And magic like yours? It doesn't vanish when a side character exits.

133. Romantic Sobriety — Detoxing from Crumb Addiction

Crumbs keep you hooked the same way bad wine does, just enough to feel it, never enough to satisfy.

They trick your heart into thinking "something" is better than "nothing."

But crumbs aren't love, they're emotional junk food.

The more you consume, the more you crave, and the weaker you feel.

Romantic sobriety is choosing *none* over "not enough."

It's blocking the breadline, deleting his name, and refusing the 2 a.m. "you up?" buffet.

Detox is hard. You'll shake. You'll miss the taste.

But soon, you'll stop craving scraps, because you'll remember you are the feast.

134. When You're Finally Bored of the Drama

One day, the late replies, the emotional cliffhangers, and the disappearing acts will stop feeling thrilling.

They'll just feel… exhausting.

You won't be mad. You won't even want revenge.

You'll just find yourself yawning at the plot twists that used to keep you up at night.

That's when you know you're done.

Because real peace isn't fireworks, it's quiet, steady, and safe.

And when drama stops being addictive, you've already won.

135. You Can Be Soft and Done

You don't have to become cold to protect yourself.

You can keep your kindness, your warmth, your softness and still refuse to be treated like an option.

Being "done" doesn't mean you slam every door and light the bridge on fire.

It can mean you quietly lock the door, draw the curtains, and choose peace over chaos.

You can love deeply and still walk away.

You can care and still close the chapter.

Soft and done is powerful, it says,

"I don't need to be hard to know my worth."

136. Finding Yourself in the Silence

At first, the quiet feels loud.

Every absence echoes. Every moment without him feels like a reminder.

Then, slowly, the noise fades.

You start hearing your own thoughts again not his voice, not his opinion, not his judgment.

In the silence, you notice things you forgot you loved:

Your morning coffee.

The way your shoulders relax when no one's picking apart your mood.

The sound of your own laughter when it's real.

Silence isn't loneliness.

It's space.

And in that space, you meet yourself again, and she's been waiting for you.

137. Healing Doesn't Have to Be Aesthetic, It Just Has to Be Honest

You don't need sunset yoga on a cliff or a colour-coordinated journal to heal.

You don't need a smoothie bowl with edible flowers, staged perfectly for Instagram.

You just need truth.

The kind that says,

"I'm not okay today,"

without a filter or a hashtag.

Healing is ugly crying at 2 a.m.

It's unwashed hair and unanswered texts.

It's doing one small thing for yourself when the big things feel impossible.

You don't have to make it pretty.

138. Stop Asking Why Wasn't I Enough? Start Asking Why Wasn't He?

You are not a puzzle missing pieces.

You are not a project in need of upgrades.

The right man doesn't make you audition for love.

He shows up ready to give it.

When you shift the question, you shift the power.

It's not, "Why wasn't I enough for him?"

It's, "Why couldn't he rise to meet me?"

Because you were always enough.

He just wasn't.

139. You Are Not a Half-Written Poem

You are not an unfinished sentence waiting for someone to complete you.

You are the whole book, plot, poetry, and punchline included.

A man can add to your story, but he cannot be the author of it.

If he walks away mid-chapter, the narrative still goes on,

and spoiler alert, it gets even better without him.

You don't need his pen to make your life worth reading.

You were always the masterpiece.

140. How to Date Yourself Before Anyone Else

Before you hand over your heart like it's a VIP pass, make sure you know what it's like to be in your own company.

Take yourself to dinner without scrolling through your phone,

book that weekend away just for you,

and stop waiting for someone to give you flowers; buy the damn bouquet.

Learn what you like, what you don't,

and what makes you feel alive outside of someone else's attention.

When you know how to love yourself first,

You stop mistaking crumbs for a feast

because you've already learned to cook for one,

and it's delicious.

141. The Power of Deleting His Name from Your Phone

It's not about being petty, it's about reclaiming your peace.

Every time his name pops up, it reopens the door you've been trying to close.

Delete it.

Not "change it to Don't Answer" or "block and still check"

delete.

Gone.

Because when you stop staring at his name,

you stop rehearsing the conversations you'll never have

and start focusing on the ones that actually matter

the ones with yourself, your friends, your future.

Sometimes the most powerful breakup tool isn't a speech,

It's the delete button.

142. You Can Miss Him Without Wanting Him Back

Missing someone doesn't mean they belong in your life.

It just means they mattered once.

You can remember the laughs, the late-night talks, the way you felt in those good moments,

without rewriting history to make him the hero.

It's okay to feel the ache and still know the truth

that you're better off without him.

Missing him is human.

Wanting better for yourself is growth.

143. Real Love Feels Safe, Not Stimulating

If it feels like a rollercoaster, it's not love, it's adrenaline.

Real love won't keep you guessing, won't spike your anxiety,

won't make you scroll through texts like they're coded messages.

It's steady. It's consistent.

It's the kind of "boring" that lets you sleep at night instead of crying at 2 a.m.

Safe isn't dull,

it's finally being able to breathe.

144. Becoming the Woman Who Never Accepts Less Again

There's a version of you who has learned every lesson,

stitched herself back together,

and now guards her peace like a dragon guards gold.

She doesn't negotiate her worth,

doesn't take "almost" when she deserves "all in,"

and never mistakes crumbs for a feast.

Once you meet her,

You'll wonder why you ever let the old you settle.

145. Protecting Your Peace Like It's Your New Job

From now on, your peace is the most valuable asset you own,

And you are its full-time security guard.

If someone tries to disturb it,

they don't get a warning,

They get walked right out of your life.

No explanations, no guilt,

Just a firm reminder to yourself that nothing is worth

losing the calm, you fought so hard to create.

146. Letting Go Doesn't Mean You Weren't Worth It

It's easy to twist a breakup into a verdict on your value,

But letting go isn't proof you failed,

It's proof you chose yourself.

He couldn't meet you where you were,

and that's not a reflection of your worth,

It's a reflection of his capacity.

Sometimes the bravest thing you'll ever do

is walking away from someone you still love,

because you finally love yourself more.

147. You Don't Need Revenge, You Need Rest

You don't have to plot some cinematic takedown

or prove how well you're doing without him.

Revenge keeps you tied to the story.

Rest sets you free from it.

Sleep in, heal slow,

and let your peace be the thing they never get access to again.

The best "you'll regret losing me"

is living so well you forget they ever did.

148. When You Start Laughing Again

One day, mid-sip of coffee or halfway through a dumb meme,

You'll hear it, your real laugh.

Not the polite one you gave him to keep the peace,

not the one you faked so he'd think you were fine.

The one that feels like sunlight breaking through your chest.

That laugh is proof.

You're not just surviving anymore.

You're coming back to life.

149. When You Can See the Crumbs and Walk Away Anyway

Healing isn't just spotting the crumbs,

It's losing all appetite for them.

You'll see the late-night "u up?"

the half-effort check-in,

the breadcrumb trail back to the same old ache…

And you won't even feel tempted.

Not because you don't remember how it felt,

but because you finally remember how *you* feel

When you choose yourself instead.

PART TEN: The Titan-Hearted Man

What a healthy, emotionally available, grown-ass man actually looks like, and how mutual respect feels when it's real.

152. He Doesn't Confuse You. He Communicates

No mixed signals. No disappearing acts. Just clarity. A titan-hearted man doesn't make you decode his messages; he tells you where you stand.

153. He Doesn't Just Text Back, He Shows Up

Replies are nice. Presence is better. He's there when it matters, not just when he's bored.

154. He Plans. He Listens. He Learns.

He doesn't "wing it" when it comes to you. He remembers what you like, plans time together, and adjusts when you tell him something matters.

155. He Makes You Feel Safe, Not Scrutinised

You can breathe around him. You can be vulnerable without bracing for criticism. Safety is his default.

156. He Wants to Know Your Mind, Not Just Your Body

Yes, he's attracted to you. But he's just as fascinated by your thoughts, opinions, and ideas.

157. He Respects Your Boundaries Without Needing a Lecture

You don't have to explain three times or justify your "no." He accepts it and doesn't punish you for it.

158. He Doesn't Love Bomb, He Loves Consistently

Grand gestures are lovely, but they don't mean much without steady, everyday care. He knows that.

159. He's Secure in Himself, Not Seeking Control

He doesn't need to diminish you to feel powerful. He wants you to shine, because he's confident in his own worth.

160. He Has Empathy, Not Just Emotions

He doesn't just feel, he cares how *you* feel, and he responds with compassion, not defensiveness.

161. He Wants Your Joy, Not Just Your Approval

He's not collecting gold stars for being a "good boyfriend." He's invested in your actual happiness.

162. He Sees the Messy Parts and Doesn't Flinch

You're human, not a highlight reel. He embraces the days you're struggling as much as the days you're thriving.

163. He Doesn't Fix You, He Stands Beside You

He knows you're not broken. You don't need repairing, you need a partner who walks with you through life's storms.

164. He Doesn't Flirt with the Line. He Honours It.

Whether it's commitment, honesty, or loyalty, he stays on the right side of the line without needing to be policed.

165. He's Not a Fantasy; He's a Man Who Chooses You Every Day

Real love isn't built on constant longing or chaos. It's in the daily choice to show up, care, and keep building together.

166. You Don't Have to Prove Your Worth. He Already Knows It.

You're not auditioning for his affection. He sees your value and treats you accordingly, always.

PART ELEVEN: Healthy Love in Real Life

Because fairytales don't always have glass slippers, but they can have mutual effort, emotional fluency, and two people actually talking.

167. Healthy Doesn't Mean Perfect, It Means Repairable

No relationship is flawless. What matters is the ability to fix the cracks without breaking each other.

168. Conflict Is Normal, Contempt Is Not

You can argue and still love each other. But the moment contempt creeps in, respect is on life support.

169. How to Disagree Without Destroying Each Other

Listen to understand, not to reload. You're solving a problem, not declaring war.

170. Holding Space for Each Other's Wounds

You don't have to heal them, but you can be a safe place while they do it themselves.

171. Emotional Labour Shouldn't Be One-Sided

One person can't carry the feelings, needs, and well-being of both. That's not love, that's burnout.

172. Sex Is Communication Too

It's not just physical. It's how you say "I see you; I want you, I cherish you" without words.

173. Love Languages Aren't a Weapon

They're meant to connect you, not to guilt-trip someone into ticking your boxes.

174. How to Grow Together Without Losing Yourself

Love should expand you, not shrink you down to fit into their comfort zone.

175. Sharing Power in the Relationship (Not One Up, One Down)

Partnership is about balance, not dominance. The scale should tip toward mutual respect.

176. How to Say I'm Wrong Without Shame

Owning mistakes builds trust. Pretending your perfect breaks it.

177. Love Is a Daily Choice - Not a Once-a-Year Grand Gesture

It's in the small, consistent acts, not just the Instagram-worthy moments.

178. Humour, Humility, and Hugs - The Holy Trinity of Real Love

If you can laugh, admit fault, and wrap each other up on bad days, you're doing it right.

179. Trust Is Earned, Built, and Rebuilt

Even healthy love has storms. What matters is how you steady the ship together.

180. You Can Be Soft Without Being Silenced

Gentleness is a strength, not an invitation to be ignored.

181. You Can Be Strong Without Dominating

Power is in protection, not in overpowering.

182. Wanting Attention Doesn't Make You Needy

It makes you human. Healthy love doesn't make you feel bad for it.

183. You Don't Need to Be Chill to Be Loved

Your feelings aren't a liability. They're part of the package.

184. Love Can Be Calm AND Passionate, Not Just One or the Other

Real love has both the peace and the spark; you shouldn't have to choose.

185. How to Be the Healthy Partner You Would Want

Bring what you expect. Don't demand what you don't deliver.

186. This Book Isn't Anti-Men, It's Anti-Crumbs

Just to slam the door on any future gingerbread-man-shaped trolls before they even finish their second passive-aggressive Goodreads review.

About the Author

Holly Symons writes like your funniest, fiercest best friend who refuses to let you text him "just one more time." She's the unapologetic voice behind *Gingerbread Man: A Girlfriend's Guide to Avoiding Men Who Breadcrumb*, helping women everywhere ditch the crumbs and demand the whole damn cake.

Known for blending sass, humour, and no-nonsense advice, Holly has turned her own misadventures in love into a roadmap for women ready to level up. She calls it "relationship rehab with a shot of espresso and a dash of glitter."

When she's not dismantling bad dating patterns with perfectly timed sarcasm, Holly can be found plotting her next book, creating Spotify playlists that double as emotional CPR, or riding off into the figurative sunset on whatever bike, metaphorical or real, takes her there.

Holly believes that self-worth isn't earned by being chosen, it's unlocked when you choose yourself first, and she's here to make sure you never settle for crumbs again.

Here's your **Gingerbread Man: No More Crumbs Spotify Playlist**

(Stay sassy, empowered, while you're driving off into the night.")

Gingerbread Man: A Girlfriend's Guide Playlist

1. **Go Your Own Way** – Fleetwood Mac
2. **Abracadabra** – Lady Gaga
3. **Irreplaceable** – Beyoncé
4. **Shout Out to My Ex** – Little Mix
5. **Since U Been Gone** – Kelly Clarkson
6. **Flowers** – Miley Cyrus
7. **Truth Hurts** – Lizzo
8. **I Will Survive** – Gloria Gaynor
9. **Shake It Off** – Taylor Swift
10. **So, What** – P!nk
11. **Don't Start Now** – Dua Lipa
12. **Before He Cheats** – Carrie Underwood
13. **Sorry Not Sorry** – Demi Lovato
14. **Woman** – Kesha
15. **Good as Hell** – Lizzo
16. **Confident** – Demi Lovato
17. **Stronger (What Doesn't Kill You)** – Kelly Clarkson
18. **No Scrubs** – TLC
19. **Unwritten** – Natasha Bedingfield
20. **About Damn Time** – Lizzo
21. **Tove Lo** – No One Dies from Love

22. **Vannessa Amorosi** – Hello Me
23. **Ashnikko** – Stupid
24. **Taylor Swift** – We are never ever getting back together
25. **Dancing In the Dark** – Bruce Springsteen

BEFORE YOU CLOSE THIS BOOK...

If anything you've read here brought up more than you expected, please remember this - you don't have to carry it alone.

Sometimes, when we start recognising crumbs for what they are, we also remember the moments we went hungry for love, respect, or kindness. That can feel heavy. If you're feeling upset, anxious, or hopeless right now, it's okay to reach out for a hand.

Here are some places to start:

AUSTRALIA – Lifeline: Call 13 11 14 or text 0477 13 11 14

USA & CANADA – 988 Suicide & Crisis Lifeline: Call or text 988

UK & IRELAND – Samaritans: Call 116 123 (freephone)

Your story isn't over. You are not alone. And just in case no one's told you today - you deserve more than crumbs. Always.

www.ingramcontent.com/pod-product-compliance
Lightning Source LLC
Chambersburg PA
CBHW071147070526
44584CB00019B/2698